The Road to Inequality

The Road to Inequality shows how policies that shape geographic space change our politics, focusing on the effects of the largest public works project in American history: the federal highway system. For decades, federally subsidized highways have selectively facilitated migration into fast-growing suburbs, producing an increasingly nonurban Republican electorate. This book examines the highway program's policy origins at the national level and traces how these intersected with local politics and interests to facilitate complex, mutually reinforcing processes that have shaped America's growing urban–suburban divide and, with it, the politics of metropolitan public investment. As Americans have become more polarized on urban–suburban lines, attitudes toward transportation policy – a once quintessentially "local" and nonpartisan policy area – are now themselves driven by partisanship, endangering investments in metropolitan programs that provide access to opportunity for millions of Americans.

CLAYTON NALL is Assistant Professor of Political Science and a faculty affiliate in the Urban Studies Program at Stanford University. His research has appeared in *The American Journal of Political Science*, *The Journal of Politics*, *Statistical Science*, and *The Lancet*, and his work has been covered by *The New York Times*, *The Washington Post*, and *The Atlantic*. This book is based on research that won the Harvard Department of Government's Toppan Prize for the best political science dissertation and the American Political Science Association (APSA) William Anderson Award for the best dissertation on federalism and state and local politics.

The Road to Inequality

How the Federal Highway Program
Polarized America and Undermined
Cities

CLAYTON NALL
Stanford University

CAMBRIDGE
UNIVERSITY PRESS

CAMBRIDGE
UNIVERSITY PRESS

University Printing House, Cambridge CB2 8BS, United Kingdom

One Liberty Plaza, 20th Floor, New York, NY 10006, USA

477 Williamstown Road, Port Melbourne, VIC 3207, Australia

314–321, 3rd Floor, Plot 3, Splendor Forum, Jasola District Centre, New Delhi – 110025, India

79 Anson Road, #06–04/06, Singapore 079906

Cambridge University Press is part of the University of Cambridge.

It furthers the University's mission by disseminating knowledge in the pursuit of education, learning, and research at the highest international levels of excellence.

www.cambridge.org
Information on this title: www.cambridge.org/9781108405492
DOI: 10.1017/9781108277952

First published 2018

Printed in the United States of America by Sheridan Books, Inc.

A catalogue record for this publication is available from the British Library.

ISBN 978-1-108-41759-4 Hardback
ISBN 978-1-108-40549-2 Paperback

To Marina

Contents

Figures

Tables

Guide to Abbreviations

AAA	American Automobile Association
AASHO	American Association of State Highway Officials
AASHTO	American Association of State Highway and Transportation Officials
AIPO	American Institute of Public Opinion
APTA	American Public Transit Association
BART	Bay Area Rapid Transit
BPR	Bureau of Public Roads
BRT	Bus Rapid Transit
CBD	Central Business District
COG	Council of Government
FHWA	Federal Highway Administration
GSS	General Social Survey
GTFS	General (or Google) Transit Feed Specification
HHFA	Housing and Home Finance Agency
HUD	Department of Housing and Urban Development
HPMS	Highway Performance Monitoring System
ISTEA	Intermodal Surface Transportation Efficiency Act of 1991
LTST	Local Transportation Sales Tax
MARTA	Metropolitan Atlanta Rapid Transit Authority
MPO	Metropolitan Planning Organization
NBI	National Bridge Inventory
NEPA	National Environmental Policy Act
NHPA	National Historic Preservation Act of 1966
NHTS	National Household Travel Survey
RTA	Regional Transit Authority
SAFETEA-LU	Safe, Accountable, Flexible, Efficient Transportation Equity Act: A Legacy for Users
STAA	Surface Transportation Assistance Act of 1982

TEA-21   Transportation Equity Act for the Twenty-first Century
TIP   Transportation Improvement Program
TARTA   Toledo Area Rapid Transit Authority
YPSPS   Youth–Parent Socialization Panel Study
ZCTA   Zip Code Tabulation Area

Acknowledgements

Any book is a result of extensive collaboration. This work has benefited from the contributions of many colleagues, experts, and friends.

Harvard University offered a methodologically diverse setting to develop a research program at the intersection of political geography and American political development. My dissertation committee of Gary King, Dan Carpenter, and Claudine Gay provided critical guidance. Under their guidance and that of other faculty members with whom I regularly met and discussed my ideas, I felt free to develop a project that did not neatly fit into one school of political science research. I was also fortunate to develop this project in the early days of the "return of geography" at Harvard University. Ryan Enos, who joined the department during my graduation year, has been a supportive peer and a great booster of political geography research. My graduate school officemate, Eitan Hersh, has become a model coauthor and colleague.

Among my colleagues in the Stanford Department of Political Science, Justin Grimmer has been a great friend and constructive critic, from the inception of this book as a dissertation prospectus at Harvard to the final stages of manuscript preparation. Nearly every piece of this manuscript has improved as a result of his advice in recent years. Paul Sniderman has been a valued mentor and an indispensable guide to the publishing process. Numerous other colleagues at Stanford read or commented on earlier drafts of the manuscript and related projects that were ultimately incorporated into this work. Karen Jusko, Jonathan Rodden, Ken Scheve, Alison McQueen, Lisa Blaydes, Lauren Davenport, Gary Segura, Terry Moe, and Bruce Cain have provided meticulous and detailed comments and publishing advice at multiple stages. A large part of Chapter 2 is a result of superb data work of Jonathan Mummolo in the course of our coauthored project on residential preferences.

Many workshop and conference participants have commented on different pieces of this project. Robert Stein, Torben Iversen, John Bullock, Rocio Titiunik, Gino Tozzi, Jim Gimpel, and Zachary Callen have served as discussants or reviewers. The material in Chapters 2 and 3 was presented at multiple job talks, and was improved by audience comments at invited talks at Yale, Ohio State, UCLA, UC-Berkeley, Oxford's Nuffield College, and Marquette University Law School.

Parts of this manuscript are excerpted and adapted from articles published in the *Journal of Politics*. I am especially grateful to the referees and editors who have evaluated and criticized the work. The blind peer review process does improve papers. Greg Caldeira at the *American Political Science Review*; Bill Jacoby at the *American Journal of Political Science*; and Jan Leighley, Jeff Jenkins, and Jennifer Merolla at the *Journal of Politics* are to be especially thanked for managing a fair review process, even when decisions were not in my favor.

A critical stage in the manuscript development was a book conference held at Stanford University in January 2016. While it was not all that difficult to convince scholars from "back east" to take a midwinter trip to California, I was fortunate to be able to assemble the so much collective wisdom and brainpower in one room. Andrea Campbell, Eric Schickler, Jeff Jenkins, Liz Gerber, and Eric Oliver offered a range of perspectives on American political development, historical survey research, urban and suburban politics, and congressional legislation that helped me focus what then existed as a sprawling survey of highways and their politics. The conference would not have been possible without generous funding from the Political Science Department and the superb organizational efforts of Eliana Vasquez. Thanks to Masha Krupenkin for helping me distill the extensive feedback from that conference.

Grant support was crucial to completion of this project. At Harvard, the Center for American Political Studies provided a year-long fellowship and seed grants, and the Taubman Center for State and Local Government provided a dissertation fellowship. At Stanford, the United Parcel Service Endowment Fund and Revs Program covered the cost of multiple online surveys and historical map research. The Institute for Research in the Social Sciences provided research fellowships, and the Vice Provost for Undergraduate Education has supported the Political Science Department's Summer Research College, an extremely generous research program, through which I have been able to hire nearly a dozen summer research assistants at no cost. That list of student assistants is a long one, but I am especially grateful to James (Jimmy) Stephens and Joseph Bourdage, who compiled the entire Roper archive series. Jonas Kemp and Nicole Dayhoff also deserve mention for their superb problem solving with map and transit data. Simon Ejdemyr and Zach O'Keeffe have put countless hours into assembling additional Rand McNally data.

Technical staff, archivists, and librarians have been vital to this project. Jeff Blossom at Harvard's Center for Geographic Analysis, Patricia Carbajales, David Medeiros, and Julie Sweetkind-Singer have been superb GIS experts. I was fortunate to get early access to Bob Berlo's bequest of state road maps and atlases to the Stanford library.

A book project would not be feasible without the willingness of experts to share their time and data to answer questions. For this, I am especially grateful to Nate Baum-Snow for sharing of his geocoded highway database. I benefited from a collaboration with Hilary Nixon and Asha Weinstein Agrawal of San José State University Mineta Transportation Institute. Richard Weingroff, who acts as the Federal Highway Administration historian and is the most productive nonuniversity scholar of modern American highway history, invited me to meet at his Federal Highway Administration office to discuss the origins of highway planning data in 2009. While this manuscript is quite critical of aspects of the federal highway program, I hope it lives up to his meticulous historical standards. Mary Graybeal, my copy editor, gave me a crash course on writing style as I completed the final manuscript for submission.

Among the faculty that I have had the privilege of learning from over the years, I owe a great debt of gratitude to the legendary Robert Booth Fowler. My first foray into political geography was as a "summer research apprentice" on Booth's Wisconsin Election Project, a long-range study of the changing voting patterns in Wisconsin's various local enclaves. Many of the partisan patterns that I learned while working on that project served as inspiration for this book.

We rarely thank those who keep other areas of our life running smoothly while we pursue our careers. I am especially thankful to Monica Hennings, who has provided loving care and tutoring to our daughter, Ingrid, while I have been finishing this project.

I have been lucky to have a family that has been incredibly supportive of my career ambitions. Carol and Lavern Nall and sister Stacy Nall Dean, have read and commented on drafts. I found the love of my life, Marina Gruber, while I was struggling through my first year on the tenure track at Stanford. In addition to keeping me grounded throughout the completion of this project, while I was finishing a final draft of the manuscript, she brought our beautiful daughter, Ingrid, into the world. Marina, I love you. Thank you for the sacrifices you've made on behalf of our family (and this book).

1 | *Introduction*

People in Cobb County don't object to upper-middle-class neighbors who keep their lawn cut and move to the area to avoid crime ... What people worry about is the bus line gradually destroying one apartment complex after another, bringing people out for public housing who have no middle-class values and whose kids as they become teenagers often are centers of robbery and where the schools collapse because the parents who live in the apartment complexes don't care that the kids don't do well in school and the whole school collapses.

> —*U.S. Rep. Newt Gingrich (R-Georgia), 1994, quoted in Merle and Earl Black, The Rise of Southern Republicans*

To progressives, the best thing about railroads is that people riding them are not in automobiles, which are subversive of the deference on which progressivism depends. Automobiles go hither and yon, wherever and whenever the driver desires, without timetables. Automobiles encourage people to think they – unsupervised, untutored, and unscripted – are masters of their fates. The automobile encourages people in delusions of adequacy, which make them resistant to government by experts who know what choices people should make.

> —*George Will, "High Speed to Insolvency: Why Liberals Love Trains," Newsweek, February 27, 2011*

In recent decades, Democrats and Republicans have become increasingly geographically polarized along urban and suburban lines and increasingly polarized around the policies that define and create metropolitan America. The ideal community of an average conservative is located in a rural or suburban area, a safe distance from what he or she perceives as urban disorder. On the other hand, an average liberal is more likely to value racial and ethnic diversity, a walkable environment, and the density of urban life (Pew Research Center, 2014). Democrats have been increasingly more likely than Republicans to live in central cities (Rodden, 2014; Nall, 2015),

1

and Democrats and Republicans have adopted increasingly different positions on *spatial policy* issues such as transit and highways. The geographic bases of the two parties have changed accordingly.

Underlying this developing spatial and political order has been *physical infrastructure*: the roads, rail lines, and utility networks that connect people in cities and beyond and sustain life in cities and suburbs alike. Regardless of where they live, Americans are "on the grid," relying on publicly subsidized highways, transit, or rail lines to get them from place to place. The development of this infrastructure has been crucial to economic opportunity, and it has also been vital to determining the residential choices of Democrats and Republicans, with significant implications for national, state, and local politics.

This book shows that the growth of suburban conservative neighborhoods, the geographic polarization of metropolitan areas, and the adverse consequences for urban Americans' mobility cannot be understood only as a result of people "voting with their feet" (e.g., "white flight"). Nor is it merely the consequence of "the car," which has had little power on its own to change residential choices. Intentionally or not, federal transportation policy has contributed to urban–suburban partisan polarization and urban–suburban inequality. By enabling Republicans' (or groups likely to become Republicans') flight to the suburbs, highways facilitated the geographic polarization of Democrats and Republicans in American metropolitan areas. This polarization has had substantial consequences for public policy attitudes and, specifically, in how transportation policy (whether pertaining to highways, mass transit, or trains) is implemented in American communities.

I center my narrative on partisan politics in order to focus on two outcomes. First, I am concerned with why the Republican Party became almost entirely a nonurban party whose voters are increasingly opposed to urban investment. Second, I am concerned with the extent to which the resulting polarized political geography has become increasingly central in the creation of policies that create and maintain metropolitan inequality and urban disinvestment. While public policy's influence on urban and suburban development has been appeared in other (often classic) works (e.g., Jackson, 1985; Fogelson, 1993, 2001; Hayden, 2003), the consequences of these policies for the *political* development of suburbs often appear as an afterthought, or is taken as a given. Partisan geography has been treated as a mere epiphenomenon of urban and suburban sprawl. But political interests in suburbia do not arise solely from the *pocketbook*, or material, interests of suburbanites. As I show, the idea of a reified "suburban interest" expressing itself in suburban bloc voting on specific policy issues has little support in survey and electoral data. When differences on transportation policy questions do emerge, they are often expressed through *partisan* disagreement. Nor can the policy attitudes of the suburbs be seen as a mere product of white flight and racial segregation. Rather, partisanship – and the geography of partisanship – are increasingly salient to the politics of mobility in metropolitan areas.

The automobile-dependent Atlanta metropolitan area – including Newt Gingrich's Cobb County – is an archetype of the urban–suburban disagreements covered in this book. The central city of Atlanta is a diversifying and Democratic city; around it are fast-growing suburbs that have, until very recently, been tagged as "Newtland" (Balz and Brownstein, 1996). Along with the rest of the suburban South, Cobb County has generally been a bulwark for the Republican Party, which now dominates the region. Like many other then-rural counties around Southern postwar cities, Cobb County was virtually unpopulated in 1960, and like so many other rural counties in the Solid South, voter turnout was low. Kennedy won 61 percent of Cobb County's 21,000 voters, and only 51 percent of Fulton County's 109,000 voters. By 2012, Cobb County's voting electorate had expanded fifteen times over, to 311,000 voters. While the county had diversified racially, it gave 55 percent of those votes to Republican Mitt Romney. By comparison, the more central and urbanized Fulton County, which has grown only by a factor of four over this period (still more than central cities in the Rust Belt), cast 64 percent of its 398,000 votes for Barack Obama. Over fifty-two years, the urban–suburban difference in the partisan vote share nearly doubled.

Many factors contributed to the development of Republican suburbs like Cobb County, and determining which of these factors is most important to partisan change is unlikely to yield any clear answer. But one feature is common to suburban areas like Cobb County: their growth and the political changes that came with that growth were a product of numerous federal investments and policies (Jackson, 1985). In this book, I examine what may be the most important of these policies: the federally financed network of highways that have made possible the development of automobile-dependent and conservative suburbs. Atlanta is one of many metropolitan areas built around modern highways. Three major Interstate highways intersect in the central city. Such radial highways extending from cities have been the infrastructure around which suburbs – and much of the modern Republican Party – have grown. For example, in Cobb County, completion of Interstate 75 in 1964 facilitated a residential boom driven in part by white flight from Atlanta (Kruse, 2005), as well as in-migration of white professionals from other US regions (Jackson, 1985). Major companies, including Martin Marietta, located their plants and corporate office parks in the "edge cities" (Garreau, 1991) along these expressways. The same suburban voters protesting the "bus line" from Atlanta might very well have been able to reach their jobs throughout the rest of Cobb County and the greater Atlanta area with ease, thanks to roads generously subsidized by the federal government.

Highways have not just facilitated the rise of Republican suburbs; they have also played a role in metropolitan inequality. The poor in Atlanta, as in other sprawling automobile-dependent metropolitan areas, have been spatially disadvantaged, facing more difficult daily commutes because of highway-induced sprawl and underinvestment in transit.[1]

Although the political (and specifically partisan) differences between cities and their peripheries have not been unique to the modern era (Glaeser and Ward, 2006), expansion of the federal-aid highway network has coincided with growing urban–suburban *partisan geographic polarization* in metropolitan areas, defined by a growing gap between the two-party vote in cities and their periphery.[2] By multiple measures, urban–suburban partisan polarization has become especially pronounced in the last fifty to sixty years, doubling since World War II and growing monotonically since 1970. Figure 1.1 presents one measure of such *geographic polarization*, the difference in the Democratic two-party vote between the central county (containing the central city) and other counties in the same Census 2000 metropolitan statistical areas (MSAs) (Leip, 2012).[3] These data, which are reported for the country as a whole and by region, show that the phenomenon of increased polarization, while most prominent in places like Atlanta, has not been limited to the South.[4] Similar patterns are observed elsewhere in the Sun Belt and in some non-Southern cities. For example, urban–suburban polarization has grown significantly in the Milwaukee area since the 1950s, much of it occurring through growth along suburban Waukesha County's I-94

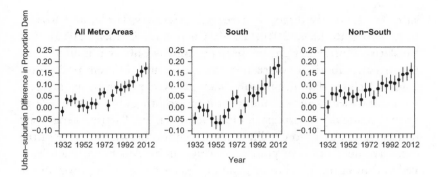

Figure 1.1. Mean metropolitan-level urban–suburban difference in the Democratic presidential vote, 1932–2012, for all metro areas (left), Southern metro areas (center), and non-Southern metro areas (right). Ninety-five percent confidence intervals for the unweighted means accompany each estimate.

Corridor. The national urban–suburban–rural political divide remains as salient as ever across the country. According to the Edison Research 2016 exit polls, rural voters supported Donald Trump by a 62–34 percent margin, while voters in cities of over fifty thousand supported Hillary Clinton by a 59–35 percent margin. Trump narrowly won the suburbs, 50 percent to 45 percent (Huang et al., 2016).

In this book, I show how infrastructure in the form of federally financed highways facilitated this geographic polarization, and what this polarization, in turn, means for the politics of mobility in metropolitan areas. I begin by explaining how transportation infrastructure has been a necessary condition of large-scale suburban growth and partisan change, facilitating migration into rural areas that were previously uninhabited and inaccessible to metropolitan commuters. I show that highways stimulated Republican growth in suburbs in many parts of the country, but especially in high-growth metropolitan areas. Metropolitan areas with more highways become more politically polarized. While infrastructure's importance to suburban development, population growth, and white flight has been explored elsewhere, my aim here is to offer here the first detailed study of its importance to the development of partisan geography and how partisan geography, in turn, shapes the politics of transportation and mobility in metropolitan areas.

Since the urban–suburban partisan gap has been consequential to numerous aspects of American politics such as legislative redistricting, just showing that highways influence partisan geography could be a sufficient scholarly discovery (see, e.g., McCarty, Poole, and Rosenthal, 2009; Rodden, 2010, 2014; Chen and Rodden, 2013). But legislative representation, while important, is only one indirect way that urban–suburban polarization translates into different policy outcomes. I show that urban–suburban partisan polarization interacts with state, local, and regional institutions to bring about more serious *spatial inequality* in American metropolitan areas. Partisan geography matters much more to equality than it might otherwise because of the extensive devolution of policy authority under American federalism. Federalism in transportation planning leaves substantial power in the hands of state and local governments and regional planning bodies – the very level at which geographic polarization is likely to be most visible and pertinent to decision-making.

By focusing on partisanship, I demonstrate why it should be more central to social science scholarship around the phenomenon of white flight and the "new suburban history." Historical scholarship (Jackson, 1985, Ch. 15) has implied that federal policies have created issue publics rooted in suburban economic and policy interests, making the problem of "automobile dependency" an important consideration. As I show, the politics of transportation policy are not quite so tidily polarized or rooted in the naively constructed understanding self-interest of urban, suburban, and rural residents. Americans across the political spectrum have in fact become increasingly dependent on cars for their daily activities, with the number of vehicle registrations rising rapidly across the postwar era (Jones, 2008). Growing cohorts of automobilists might, as a result, be expected to demand additional roadbuilding. Similarly, among the mostly poor and elderly Americans without automobile access, one might expect to see much higher support for transit. Other scholarship on suburbia has suggested that "suburban" interests may reflect little more than white interest in protecting and maintaining neighborhoods (McGirr, 2001; Kruse, 2005; Hayward, 2013). Newt Gingrich's opposition to the "bus line" running into the suburbs could reasonably be interpreted as a statement of just that sort of "defensive localism" by white suburbanites (Weir, 1996).

While race and economic interest are deeply connected with partisanship, survey data show that partisan identity has become associated with support for policies designed to support urban mobility, even after accounting for respondents' race, income, and place of residence. These policy attitudes do not fit the stereotypes of prohighway suburbanites and antihighway urbanites, They do show that partisans disagree over whether to spend money on *alternatives* to highways. On surveys, both Republicans and Democrats have expressed strong support for building and funding highways, and this support does not appear to be driven only by naive economic self-interest (as captured by regular use of highways or vehicle mileage). Even urban voters have been generally supportive of highway spending, perhaps because they are, according to survey data reported in Chapter 4, *more* likely than rural voters to use an expressway, or because they do not see the harm of investing in widely used highways.[5] When Republicans and Democrats do disagree over transportation, partisanship appears to be as strong an explanation as race, income, or density of place of residence.

While one must be careful not to read too much from regression analyses of survey questions asked about unfamiliar or low-salience policies (Converse, 1970; Bartels, 2003), one reason for growing partisan disagreement on transportation policy may be the transmission of important signals from party elites to both elected officials and the engaged partisan public. Among party activists (whose views are often injected into party platforms), the partisan fissure over transportation policy has been especially pronounced. For example, while the Democratic Party platform has featured a pro-urban and pro-density approach to transportation and urban planning, the 2012 and 2016 Republican platforms accused the Democrats of pro-urban "social engineering" (Republican Party, 2012, 2016). In short, what seem to be growing differences over transportation policy are manifesting in a more pronounced way among engaged partisans.

These growing partisan differences might be expected to influence the behavior of responsive partisan officials. Yet these partisan differences among voters and activists have been slow to translate into policy change, at least at the federal level: highway bills have maintained approximately the same distribution of funding for highways and highway alternatives (such as transit) for about forty years. And, importantly, almost all of this funding is distributed in the form of matching funds to state governments, where local biases determine project allocation.[6] Even as the federal government has become more involved in transportation, decisions over the distribution of transportation funding are still largely made by state and local governments, as they have since the earliest days of the Republic (Weingast and Wallis, 2005). Formula-allocated federal surface transportation funds are delivered to state and local governments. This is the very level at which the geographic distribution of partisans and their preferences is likely to matter most. The longstanding devolution of transportation programs to state and local institutions exposes policy to a host of local biases, including those arising from the urban–suburban partisan geographic divide.[7]

Why Examine Highways' Role in Geographic Polarization?

This book begins by demonstrating the federal highway program's role in the polarization of metropolitan areas, and the implications of this polarization for the subsequent development of American transportation policy. Since 1916, the federal government has delivered federal matching funds to states to build rural roads, major intercity routes, and the expressways of the Interstate Highway System. By influencing Americans' residential choices and changing the geographic distribution of increasingly ideological partisans, the federal highway program has created new, more polarized communities. As highways have made metropolitan areas more polarized, they have introduced conflict over an array of distributive and redistributive policies, with transportation policy being one of the most important. In the process, highways have also created political conditions that have worsened urban–suburban *spatial inequality*.[8]

To explain exactly why metropolitan areas have become polarized, one would need to consider many separate and sometimes mutually dependent causes. Instead of attempting to identify the "causes of effects," offering a survey of all the contributing factors to suburbanization and urban-suburban polarization, here I aim to focus on the "effects of causes" (Holland, 1988). While urban–suburban polarization has had many causes, ample reason existo estimate highways' effect on American metropolitan areas' political geography. To identify highways' effects, I examine the Interstate Highway System, which dwarfed previous federal investments in highways. Since passage of the Federal Aid Highway Act of 1956, the federal highway program has been a massive spatial intervention that remade American metropolitan areas. However, until now, social scientists especially have treated it mostly as historical background to the major demographic and political changes in metropolitan areas across the postwar period. Despite their enormous scale – the federal government has spent in excess of $1 trillion in present-day dollars on highway grants to state governments since 1957 – highways and other transportation infrastructure usually receive only passing mention in political science research on residential segregation and urban–suburban inequality.[9] One reason for the neglect is that infrastructure's influence over suburban development is seen as common sense. Indeed, some effects of highways, such as their direct effects on mobility and their less direct effects on suburban development, may seem "ex post obvious." But the specific mechanisms by which highways have influenced the political development of American metropolitan areas have rarely been developed in political science research, at least beyond this basic intuition.[10]

Unlike impacts of other policies that have reshaped the suburbs, highways' effects can be plausibly inferred from both historical and contemporary data. Among the most important reasons for studying the federal highway program is that it has been a massive policy that lends itself to causal analysis. A federal formula-based matching program has subsidized road building on designated federal-aid highways since 1916, beginning with the Federal Aid Road Act of 1916. Over most of this period, across most types of highway mileage, the federal government reimbursed state highway departments building roads by reimbursing half (or more) of construction costs. The program's annual outlays increased greatly under the Federal-Aid Highway Act of 1956, which launched the Interstate Highway System as we know it today, created a Highway Trust Fund supported by gas taxes, and covered 90 percent of the cost of Interstate routes (in addition to funding other federal-aid roads). Before passage of the 1956 act, the federal government provided total federal-aid highway funding of only $6.2 billion per year (in 2016 dollars). This amount leapt to $20–25 billion by the early 1960s as states quickly built Interstate projects to claim their share of federal funding (United States. Department of Transportation. Federal Highway Administration. Office of Highway Information Management, 1996, HF-210). In brief, the reasons for studying the federal highway program as a central cause of suburbanization and polarization of metropolitan areas are threefold: it has been a large-magnitude intervention, it is a clear case of devolved federal policy interacting with political geography within states, and, finally, the highway program lends itself to careful causal analysis in ways that other federal policies do not.

The Federal Highway Program Is a Massive Spatial Intervention

A key reason to be concerned with the federal highway program's political effects is the program's sheer magnitude. Especially after passage of the Federal Aid Highway Act of 1956, generous aid drawn from the Highway Trust Fund helped to create what was to be, at the time, the largest public works project in history.[11] Between 1957 and 2010, the Highway Trust Fund disbursed over $1.4 trillion (in 2010 dollars) to state highway and transportation departments (Williamson, 2012, 12).[12] Federal highway dollars go to different classes of highways in the federal-aid system, but the Interstate program alone had a huge impact on American geography and American life. Interstates required excavation of 42 billion tons of dirt, the equivalent of 116 Panama Canal projects (McNichol, 2006, 126). Making room for Interstates also required clearing urban neighborhoods, such that the localized damage wrought by the project was immense. In the process of creating the highway right-of-way urban communities, Interstates displaced a roughly estimated one million persons, often in poor and ethnically and racially diverse neighborhoods (Mikulski, 1970; Mohl, 1993; Mohl, 2002, 2). Since Interstate highways have become a commonplace feature of daily life, their behavioral effects have been as extensive: Americans today drive more than 750 billion vehicle-miles per year on Interstate highways, and through 2014 had cumulatively driven 32 trillion vehicle miles (Cox and Love, 1996, 5; United States. Department of Transportation. Research and Innovative Technologies Administration's Bureau of Transportation Statistics, 2017). The federal-aid highway program has not just been a major construction program, but a major presence in Americans' daily life.

The Federal Highway Program Reveals the Challenges of Policy Federalism

The magnitude of the highway program is reason enough to study its wide-ranging effects, but the program's institutional design has also been important to the creation of both metropolitan geography and the geographically contingent political institutions that are sensitive to polarized political geography. The federal-aid highway program put implementation of federal transportation policy goals in the hands of state governments and their subdivisions, where conflicts over transportation policy typically arise. The importance of this level of policy implementation has sometimes been neglected in existing work on the federal politics of transportation. While political scientists have generally focused on the congressional distributive politics of highways, usually to test legislative theories (e.g., Evans, 1994, 2004; Lee, 2003), this approach leaves unanswered the equally important question of how and where states use their federal highway money when they get it. Institutionally, the federal-aid highway program is structured much like Medicaid, the federally subsidized medical assistance program administered by the states. Like Medicaid, the federal-aid highway program operates through formula-based matching payments (Mitchell, 2016; Michener, 2018), leaving states to oversee the programs according to federal standards. Just as states have substantial discretion over Medicaid program administration, they also decide where and how to apply federal transportation project dollars (within prescribed limits). While federal highway bills and associated regulations set rules on building and contracting standards–coordinated by the American Association of State Highway and Transportation Officials (AASHTO) – highway construction and contracting remain an overwhelmingly state-based responsibility at the mercy of state-level politics.

This basic federal-aid program has persisted through more than a century of highway program expansions and reforms. The formula-based funding first passed under the Federal Aid Road Act of 1916 has grown in complexity, but the fundamentals of the program have changed only incrementally as national transportation needs have evolved (*The Federal Aid Road Act, Summary of the*, 1916). At multiple points, presidents have pursued alternatives to the formula-based program, and have invariably faced challenges from existing interests, particularly from the state and federal highway officials with a stake in the status quo. Understanding this history is key to understanding the persistence of the program and its effects on state-level transportation policy. The history also sheds light on why state-level geography would play a larger role in the politics of mobility in metropolitan areas.

The first president to propose major reforms to the federal-aid highway program was Franklin Roosevelt, whose role in the development of the American highways is often underappreciated. As more

Americans drove automobiles and truck transportation became more important to commerce, the need for a national express highway network became increasingly obvious. As early as 1935, President Roosevelt had expressed interest in a national scale "superhighway" program consisting of multiple cross-country expressways (Goddard, 1994, 158–61). Roosevelt's interest in a system of national expressways funded by tolls differed from existing policy in two respects: it involved a national network requiring national, versus state-level, planning, and it also would have departed from the existing federal-aid program by employing toll financing (Williamson, 2012, 6). State and federal highway bureaucrats resisted this idea. A commissioned report titled *Toll Roads and Free Roads* authored by highway engineers in the federal Bureau of Public Roads labeled such a system economically infeasible, temporarily halting the exploration of policy alternatives (United States. Bureau of Public Roads, 1939).

During World War II, planning for postwar highways continued apace, resulting in a new proposal for a national expressway system in *Interregional Highways* (United States, Public Roads Administration, 1944), which served as the first rough draft proposal of what would become Interstate Highway System. When Congress adopted the proposal in the Federal-Aid Highway Act of 1944, it authorized a system of 40,000 miles of roads. However, the legislation preserved most aspects of the existing federal-aid program, including the existing 50-percent matching ratio for federal-aid roads, including routes on the Interstate system. As a result, few states had an incentive to build the highest-quality Interstate expressways envisioned in the legislation.

Beginning in 1954, President Eisenhower addressed the shortcomings of existing legislation, commissioning a blue-ribbon committee led by Gen. Lucius Clay (Ret.), to explore development and financing options for a new express highway program (Weingroff, 2015). The committee's initial proposal suggested a new highway financing system far from the status quo: a federal highway authority with bond-issuing powers – a reform that, if implemented, would have created a new funding source distinct from both congressional appropriations and state governments. This proposal failed in Congress amid concerns over increasing debt and declining congressional control. In its place, Sen. Albert Gore (D-TN) and Rep. George Fallon (D-MD) sponsored a bill to expand and increase funding for the existing federal-aid matching program. This Democratic counterproposal, which passed after a year-long delay driven by a minor controversy over financing, created a new federal fuel tax to finance a Highway Trust Fund that would cover 90 percent of the construction costs of Interstate routes. The Federal Aid Highway Act of 1956 provided states an incentive to build expensive expressways across their metropolitan areas. While the legislation created new standards for highway construction and envisioned a single national system, it substantially preserved states' powers over highway construction (Patashnik, 2000; Rose and Mohl, 2012, ch. 7).

Correctly regarded as landmark legislation that funded the largest public works project in American history (and in world history up to that point, by some measures), the Federal Aid Highway Act of 1956 also further entrenched a status quo in which American surface transportation policy is built around generous "highway bills" that deliver funding to states for their preferred projects. The basic federal-aid relationship established in successive highway bills has remained robust ever since, even as liberal activist groups, fiscal conservatives, and other critics have attacked the program over the years and diverted "highway" funds to other transportation purposes. Urban residents and environmentalists threatened completion of the Interstate program in the late 1960s and early 1970s, leading to reforms that constrained highway construction programs, but the general structure of the federal-aid program remained robust as highway critics joined with highway advocates to develop a joint highway-transit transportation program.

By the early 1970s, "Freeway Revolts" had arisen in many cities, halting the construction of several dozen controversial expressway segments and seemingly putting the national highway program in political jeopardy (Mohl, 2004). States with blocked segments were not permitted to convert apportioned highway funding to other uses (Altshuler and Luberoff, 2003, 87–90). However, cities with struggling urban transit and rail systems saw the Highway Trust Fund as an ideal funding source. Earlier mass transportation legislation, the Urban Mass Transportation Act of 1964, had delivered only $750 million in general revenue to bolster financially distressed urban transit systems. Under the Federal-Aid Highway Act of 1973, advocates of federal urban transit funding succeeded in obtaining a provision to allow states to convert a portion of their unused highway funding to use on mass transit projects (Altshuler and Luberoff, 2003, 188–9). Protransit representatives, many of them from northeastern states and liberal urban centers, won a legislative victory that also unintentionally reinforced the highway funding status quo. As Patashnik (2000) notes, this measure tethered urban, nonhighway transportation alternatives to the Highway Trust Fund and to the federal transportation aid system.[13] Since the 1970s, trust fund outlays have been split between highways and transit approximately on an 80–20 basis, a rule that persisted through the 2015 FAST Act surface transportation bill (Laing, 2015*a*, *b*).

The 1970s highway-transit bargain gave urban representatives a reason to maintain the Highway Trust Fund and support highway bills that continued to favor suburban and rural interests (Patashnik, 2000, 122). As the problems of this transportation policy devolution have become more obvious, federal reformers have appeared to draw the wrong lessons from the history of the federal-aid program. In fact, as I demonstrate in Chapter 5, efforts to devolve program responsibility even further – to metropolitan planning organizations (MPOs) – have left transportation planning even more sensitive to local preferences and biases, including those arising from urban–suburban polarization.

The history of federal highway aid shows that efforts to reform federal transportation policy have sometimes succeeded in changing transportation priorities in favor of urban transportation interests, but they rarely disturb states' basic discretion over transportation planning and priorities. As a result, transportation policy remains vulnerable to state and metro-area politics that highways themselves helped to create.

The Federal Highway Program Was a Clear and Measurable Intervention

While the federal highway program is important as an example of a large spatial policy intervention implemented in the context of policy federalism, a final reason to study highways is that we can convincingly estimate their effect. Major federally financed highways have been a discrete, easily measured, and plausibly exogenous spatial intervention. Collectively, these factors make federally financed highways an ideal test case of the ways spatial policies affect behavior, political geography, and the implementation of public policies.

One reason to study highways is that they are an observable intervention. The history of the placement of road networks is readily available in the public record, such that one can look back at the development of road networks over decades. While the beneficiaries of social welfare and tax expenditure programs tend to be anonymous, their participation in the programs often lost to history, the location of highways, railroads, and canals can be discerned from historical atlases available on the shelves of any major map library (Atack, 2013; Ejdemyr, Nall, and O'Keeffe, 2015) or, occasionally, from published and more detailed public infrastructure databases (Baum-Snow, 2007*a*). While tracking the flow of transportation dollars through the federal-aid system is difficult, we do know where and when highways have been built over the past century, and data on the construction of the Interstate Highway System, especially, have been well documented and exploited by researchers (e.g., Baum-Snow, 2007*a*). In the case of the Interstate Highway System, the assignment mechanism – the rationale for building the system and the factors used to determine where highways should be built – was laid out by policy planners in *Interregional Highways* and in subsequent policy documents (Rubin, 1991; Nall, 2015). With knowledge of the highway-planning process in hand, one can more plausibly estimate highways' causal effect on a host of outcomes including metropolitan political geography.

An Outline of the Book

My argument proceeds in three interrelated parts. First, I show how highways changed the geographic distribution of partisans by facilitating residential sorting. Second, I demonstrate why the geographic distribution of partisans is significant to the development of transportation policy, drawing upon survey data on transportation attitudes and data on metropolitan institutions that manage transportation policy. Finally, I consider how partisan geographic polarization interacts with policy federalism to worsen spatial inequality, delivering transportation policies that disadvantage urbanized areas and the transit-dependent.

Beginning in Chapter 2, I demonstrate why highways have been so important to the geographic distribution of partisans. I show that highways facilitate sorting through two key mechanisms.

First, highways can be understood as a *catalyst* of residential sorting: they accelerate migration that would not have occurred but for the improved transportation infrastructure. While there is nothing inherent in highways that makes people more Republican, or leads Republican-leaning groups to move to the suburbs, highways facilitated suburban development at a time when Republicans (and groups in the process of converting to the Republican Party) were more likely to migrate to the suburbs. The mobility provided by highways was especially valuable to white and middle-class Americans, who could access suburbs in which zoning and restrictive covenants excluded the urban poor and racial minorities (Danielson, 1976). Highways were not a primary cause of this suburban exclusion, but they did facilitate migration of groups that could take advantage of it. These beneficiaries of exclusion were more likely to be white and middle class and to become Republican.

Even where housing options have not been limited by discriminatory local policies, highways have allowed Democrats and Republicans to act on their divergent residential preferences. For more than forty years, surveys have shown that Republicans have been more likely than Democrats to prefer suburbs and rural areas (e.g., Gallup Organization, 1983; Pew Research Center, 2014). Increasing household mobility potentially allowed partisans to act on these divergent preferences over type of place (urban versus nonurban); racial composition; and, among some Americans, the partisan context of their community (Mummolo and Nall, 2017). By acting on these preferences, American partisans sorted geographically.

Second, highways act as a *filter*, as they facilitate greater mobility among higher socioeconomic-status groups that can afford to make the most extensive use of automobiles and highways. While the poor often have access to automobiles, they are more likely than the rich to rely on walking, buses, or light rail (Pucher and Renne, 2003).

These two mechanisms have not gone unnoticed among the "developer-entrepreneurs" responsible for creating new suburbs (Burns, 1994), and who heavily influence local land-use policy (Molotch, 1976).[14] Real estate developers often follow transportation infrastructure when building new housing projects, anticipating the housing demand that will arise along transportation corridors (Warner, 1978). At midcentury, these developers were building new "restricted" housing in areas adjoining new expressways. They often promoted the exclusivity of suburbia and its accessibility by convenient freeway travel.

After demonstrating how highways influence the behavior of households and developers to facilitate sorting, I show in Chapter 3 that an important consequence has been the partisan geographic polarization of American metro areas. Exploiting exogenous variation in the timing and location of construction of the Interstate Highway System, I show that Interstates made suburban counties where they were built more Republican over time. Consistent with the results in Chapter 2, a key mechanism by which highways facilitated this residential sorting was by enabling additional localized growth in suburban counties in already fast-growing regions. In metropolitan areas that were already growing (as captured by metropolitan population change between 1950 and 1960), highways facilitated a substantial pro-Republican shift. (At the same time, suburbs in low-growth or negative-growth areas, mostly in the Rust Belt, either shifted to the Republicans to a lesser degree and sometimes became more Democratic.) The Republican shift was especially pronounced in, but by no means exclusive to, the South, where highways facilitated suburban growth in the suburban peripheries of fast-growing metropolitan areas like Atlanta. As I show, these effects took root at a critical moment, as northern Republicans were migrating to the region and white Southern Democrats were realigning into the Republican Party (Shafer and Johnston, 2006). At the same time, large metropolitan areas with more Interstate highways became more polarized along urban–suburban lines than they would have been otherwise.

I then assess how this matters for public attitudes toward transportation policy. Because programs like transportation are developed and distributed by place, we might expect people to form attitudes toward spending on highways and transit based on a set of personal household economic factors associated with the population density or urban development in their place of residence. More specifically, their policy attitudes might be in response to their personal reliance on specific transportation modes (e.g., automobiles versus public transit) associated with different levels of urbanization. However, if partisans are generally becoming more ideologically consistent, with Democrats becoming more consistently liberal and Republicans more consistently conservative on multiple policy issues, then one might expect attitudes to vary by geography merely because ideologically consistent Democrats and Republicans have sorted into different places.

In Chapter 4, I address the question of place-based policy attitudes using historical survey evidence from the Roper Center for Public Opinion Research, as well as more recent, original survey results on partisans' attitudes toward spending on highways and other transportation alternatives. I find that partisanship has become increasingly associated with transportation attitudes. This means that the partisan geography of cities and suburbs, as much as personal interests or reliance on specific transportation policies, may explain urban–suburban polarization on seemingly place-dependent policy items like highway and transit spending. Highway spending has generally received strong bipartisan support, but Democrats and Republicans have diverged over how to allocate transportation spending, especially for mass transit projects and programs. In a set of original survey results that feature much more fine-grained geographic data than are typically available, I find that population density, and even race and income, typically do little to explain attitudes on transportation policy beyond what can be captured by partisanship. While this result does not demonstrate that race, income, or place of residence are unimportant, it does show that partisanship is now anchoring policy attitudes on transportation policy questions that previously elicited bipartisan support.

To the extent that partisans are taking on more ideologically consistent positions (sorting ideologically) on the question of transportation funding and have also been moving into distinct places (geographically sorting), we might expect to find partisan politicians adopting more extreme positions on transportation issues. Chapter 5 demonstrates that partisan geographic polarization does matter, though I find that this polarization is most consequential not in Congress, which has been the focus of so much polarization research, but at the metropolitan level. Even as Republicans have become an almost exclusively suburban and rural party, transportation policy outcomes have barely changed. In fact, the congressional politics of transportation policy have been surprisingly devoid of active public conflict. Disagreements have arisen in the context of writing the "highway bill" but these disagreements rarely manifest themselves in roll call votes (Adler and Wilkerson, 2015).[15] Logrolling and the norm of universalism in the distribution of pork-barrel projects tend to smooth over conflict, especially in a policy area like transportation, which allows for easy horse-trading of specific projects (Weingast,

1979; Evans, 1994, 2004). While urban and rural interests have intermittently battled in Congress over highway and transit funding, neither growing urban–suburban polarization nor changes in party control of Congress and the presidency have substantially changed the federal transportation funding status quo since 1973.[16]

Polarized metropolitan political geography becomes much more important, and visible, at the geographic level at which transportation policy is implemented. By delivering funding while allowing state and local governments discretion over their highway and transit programs, federal transportation policy has migrated implementation of transportation policy to the very setting in which geographic polarization is most likely to be consequential. I show how urban–suburban polarization is likely to worsen antiurban bias in the implementation of transportation policy in metropolitan areas. With metropolitan planning organizations (MPOs) given more power under a 1991 transportation bill, more transportation planning is now done at the metropolitan level by regional governing boards on which suburban communities enjoy disproportionate voting power (Sanchez, 2006). Combined with urban–suburban polarization, this means that suburban, and more Republican, opponents of urban transportation investments such as mass transit are better able to block spending on projects typically preferred by urban Democrats.[17] The increasing importance of partisanship becomes especially clear whenever voters have a direct say on local and regional transportation questions through the initiative and referendum process in local and regional initiatives and referenda: precincts populated by Democrats are more likely to cast votes in support of transit and other urban transportation investments. I examine the relationship between the two-party vote and votes on precinct-level transit referenda conducted in 2016 in two quite different metropolitan areas: San Francisco and Detroit. The vote for such measures is so tightly correlated with the two-party Democratic vote that such votes look like purely partisan affairs. If population density, racial attitudes, or personal dependence on transit influences the public's votes on transportation measures, these differences are today subsumed by partisanship.

I conclude with a discussion of the implications for American inequality and the development of transportation in metropolitan areas. Income inequality has become a central line of inquiry in political science. Unequal political participation, congressional polarization, and dysfunctional representative democracy have all been tied to income and racial inequality (see, e.g., American Political Science Association Task Force on Inequality and American Democracy, 2004; and McCarty, Poole, and Rosenthal, 2006). My results highlight how transportation policy has contributed to both geographic polarization and inequality in metropolitan areas. One contribution of this study is to emphasize that metropolitan issues that have commonly been discussed primarily in terms of the racial and economic segregation have become increasingly bound up with partisan politics. Even seemingly local and bipartisan matters such as transportation policy are becoming more tightly associated with partisanship. In turn, the geographic distribution of partisans dictates how their attitudes influence locally consequential policies.

My account outlines the unintended consequences that arise at the intersection of place-making policies, policy federalism, and political geography. Federal highway policy did not just help to create suburbs. It also facilitated the sorting of Americans on urban–suburban lines. In the process, growing partisan divisions over public policy are more likely to manifest themselves in urban–suburban conflict carried out in local governments and metropolitan-level institutions. As partisanship becomes more predictive of policy attitudes, partisans' geographic distribution will become more important in determining policy outcomes. The federal highway program has paved the way to partisan polarization and increased metropolitan inequality.

Notes

1 A strong correlate of intergenerational income mobility is the proportion of workers with commutes under 15 minutes. The Atlanta area, which ranks forty-ninth out of fifty in terms of intergenerational income mobility, also has one of the nation's worst commuting environments. In 2000, only 18 percent of workers in the Atlanta Commuting Zone had commutes of under 15 minutes (Chetty et al., 2014; Online Supplemental Data, Commuting Zone Characteristics). Workers' long automobile commutes are a result of highway infrastructure facilitating the spread of jobs into the suburbs, making job access more challenging.

2 In one of many examples of cities' conflict with their peripheries, Tammany Hall's George Washington Plunkitt famously berated the "hayseed" legislators in Albany who declined to fund projects in patronage-ridden New York City (Riordan, 1995; Burns et al., 2009).

Many studies have examined political differences between cities and their peripheries, including Hawley (1956). Teaford (1979) examines metropolitan fragmentation, while Gainsborough (2001) examines the development of suburban conservatism using individual-level survey data.

3 These graphs include present-day MSAs with at least one central city of at least two hundred thousand persons.

4 Various alternative measures of residential segregation in the two-party vote, including the dissimilarity index (Massey and Denton, 1988), yield similar results.

5 Of course, rural residents are more likely to drive than to bike, walk, or take transit to work (Pisarski, 2006). One reason for their lack of reliance on expressways is that they use local, non-express highways.

6 About 20 percent of the Highway Trust Fund has been assigned to mass transit funding since the mid-1970s under an ongoing, bipartisan understanding (Congressional Budget Office, 2015).

7 Policy devolution exposes program constituents to localized biases and highly variable program administration. See Mettler (1998), Katznelson (2005, 2013), and Michener (2018).

8 For a recent discussion of the concept of spatial inequality, see Weir (2014). See also Wilson (1987, 1996); Rae (2001); and Lobao, Hooks, and Tickamyer (2007).

9 Unless otherwise indicated, inflation adjustments were performed using the Bureau of Labor Statistics Inflation Calculator (United States. Bureau of Labor Statistics, 2016).

10 The federal surface transportation programs, which provide generous grants to state governments, create perverse fiscal incentives, oversubsidizing capital spending, and inducing states to "gold-plate" their highway programs, an instance of the more general moral hazard problem in fiscal federalism (Peterson, 1995; Rodden, 2006). As a result, states spent more on highways than they would have otherwise.

11 There is some dispute over what constitutes a single "public works project." The Interstate Highway System (originally planned as a 41,000-mile network) has since been eclipsed by China's National Trunk Highway System (see, e.g., Faber, 2014).

12 Accounting for diversion of trust fund dollars to transit the Federal Aid Highway Act of 1973, approximately $1.2 trillion of that amount went to roads.

13 The Surface Transportation Assistance Act (STAA) of 1982 increased the gas tax by 9 cents, diverting 1 cent of the money raised into a Mass Transit Account in the Highway Trust Fund (Patashnik, 1997).

14 See also Weiss (1987).

15 According to data assembled by Adler and Wilkerson (2014), the number of stand-alone transportation bills introduced, let alone brought to the floor, has dropped substantially since the Federal Aid Highway Act of 1973.

16 This is not to suggest that the status quo has gone unchallenged, especially from the right. To cite two current examples at the time of this writing, in 2015, Rep. Mark Sanford (R-SC) and Rep. Thomas Massie (R-KY), who sit at the most conservative end of the House Republican Caucus, proposed eliminating Trust Fund transit support on the grounds that road users should recoup all the benefits of the federal gas tax (Massie, 2015). Such statements were echoed in the 2016 Republican Party platform (Republican Party, 2016).

17 For discussion of the influence of communities' partisan composition on the formation of intergovernmental boards, see Gerber, Henry, and Lubell (2013). See also An and Bostic (2017).

2 | *How Highways Facilitate Partisan Geographic Sorting*

In this chapter, I show that highways have been the sine qua non of modern suburban growth and the associated partisan geographic sorting observed during the postwar period. I outline the mechanisms by which highways facilitate the type of development that leads to urban–suburban polarization. I demonstrate that highways do more to shape metropolitan geography than merely facilitate suburban population growth and urban population decline. Highways have shaped metropolitan poltical geography in two ways: catalyzing residential migration and filtering migration by selectively providing mobility throughout metropolitan areas. First, highways play a role as a *catalyst* of Americans' divergent residential preferences. They have exogenously increased the daily travel range of automobile users, providing them a larger set of neighborhoods to choose from to match their residential preferences. Where local housing policy is economically or racially exclusionary, highways have facilitated the selective migration of groups that are able to live in suburban neighborhoods, exacerbating the adverse effects of local exclusionary policies.[1] Second, highways act as a *filter* on residential migration and selection, providing direct mobility improvements to automobile users and fewer mobility advantages to those who lack automobiles or rely on transit.

Of course, race, income, and partisanship are correlated, and highways facilitate urban–suburban sorting on all three of these variables, which may lead some readers to ask whether partisan sorting and geographic polarization are nothing more than a second-order effect of racial and socioeconomic sorting. Only the causes of racial and income segregation have previously been analyzed in any depth, while partisan segregation is often treated as a secondary consequence of the other two. Scholars across multiple disciplines have demonstrated that highways facilitated "white flight." For example, modern urban and suburban history scholarship often refers to the role of expressways in suburban growth and migration (e.g., Jackson, 1985, 249–50; Cohen, 2004, 196–99; Kruse, 2005, 243–44). Recent work in urban economics has carefully estimated how highways facilitated suburban population growth (e.g., Baum-Snow, 2007*a*, *b*). While these diverse studies have linked Interstate highways to white flight in the postwar period, they rarely have addressed how partisan geography has changed as a result. Although even committed partisans are rarely motivated specifically by the partisan composition of possible neighborhoods or communities, highways facilitate sorting on other characteristics on which partisans disagree, leading to greater partisan segregation (Cho, Gimpel, and Hui, 2012; Hui, 2013; Gimpel and Hui, 2015; Mummolo and Nall, 2017).

Transportation's Role in Segregation and Sorting

Analyses of the origins of residential segregation have tended to focus on two divergent models of segregation, neither of which explicitly incorporates transportation's role in metropolitan residential change.[2] Under one paradigm, segregation of various types is explained as the aggregate consequence of individual choices. In the second, segregation is regarded as a product of discriminatory practices and policies constructed to reinforce segregation (Massey and Denton, 1993; Rothstein, 2017).

   Much of what we know about the causes of residential segregation has been developed by scholars of racial and economic segregation, who have focused on the aggregate consequences of individual sorting behavior resulting from people exercising their personal preferences in open housing markets. One approach to segregation, widely described as the "Schelling model," suggests that segregation can arise from a small proportion of individuals acting on only modest preferences for neighborhoods that match their own type (Schelling, 1971*a*).[3] Thus, "micromotives" in the form of household preferences may lead to "macrobehavior" in the form of segregated housing (Schelling, 1971*b*). Such individual sorting, it has been argued, can occur on the basis of cultural and political preferences. A recent popular book, *The Big Sort*, holds that different preferences related to population density, neighborhood social characteristics, and cultural features may drive partisans into more politically compatible neighborhoods (Bishop and Cushing, 2008; Hui, 2013; Gimpel and Hui, 2015). For example, young, unmarried, or secular voters, are more likely than older, married, or religious voters to be Democrats and prefer urban life (see also Pew Research Center, 2014). Local governments have, in turn, provided baskets of goods and services to compete for preferred resident types (Tiebout, 1956).

A competing explanation of the causes of segregation suggests that individual-level sorting models inadequately capture the importance of governmental and private-sector discrimination in housing markets. Private and public housing discrimination (e.g., Yinger, 1986), redlining (e.g., Hillier, 2003), and economically and racially exclusionary zoning (Danielson, 1976; Massey and Denton, 1993) influence the economic and racial composition of neighborhoods. Because this discrimination is based on factors that are correlated with partisanship, economic and racial discrimination also have important consequences for partisan residential sorting.

Although transportation infrastructure appears in these accounts of sorting and segregation, it has rarely been treated as a central driver of segregation and sorting.[4] Here, I discuss transportation infrastructure's multifaceted contributions to residential segregation. Transportation infrastructure facilitates sorting and segregation in two ways: as a *catalyst* for household-level preferences and as a *filter* that selectively facilitates mobility on the basis of income, automobile ownership, and related factors. Both of these mechanisms have consequences for communities' changing political makeup.

Foremost, transportation infrastructure should be understood as a *catalyst* of residential preferences and options, expanding households' access to existing community and housing options. As a chemical catalyst enables reactions between reactants, so transportation infrastructure enables households to reside in communities that would have been inaccessible (due to daily travel time or costs) in the infrastructure's absence. Infrastructure allows them to choose from among a wider array of residential options, acting on their preferences with no loss of utility relative to a status quo lacking good transportation infrastructure. Just by enabling households to act on their preferences more easily, transportation infrastructure may increase residential sorting.[5]

How transportation infrastructure catalyzes residential preferences therefore depends on local conditions. For example, where suburbs have nondiscriminatory housing policies and economically diversified housing options, transportation infrastructure could facilitate migration leading to residential integration. More often, transportation occurs in and around localities that impose *de jure* or de facto constraints on residential choice, whether through restrictive zoning or private development and housing practices that have a disparate economic or racial impact. Highways and other transportation infrastructure expand residential options, but only to the extent that households have options to exercise. In the absence of such options, highways will tend to exacerbate ongoing segregation and sorting.

Transportation infrastructure also acts as a *filter*: different transportation modes have different user demographics, which contribute to varied residential settlement patterns. Personal automobiles, commuter rail, light rail, and city bus service each serve different socioeconomic and racial groups, with different implications for filtering. Automobile and commuter rail passengers, for example, tend to be more affluent than bus riders. Household transportation costs including automobile operating expenses, tolls, and fares, can contribute to economic sorting of transportation mode user bases, indirectly resulting in partisan differences. For example, commuter rail users have typically had higher incomes than users of other surface transportation modes, such that investing in commuter rail lines may facilitate economic segregation by enabling easier commuting between more affluent suburban neighborhoods (or urban residences) and commercial districts. In contrast, city bus riders have had the lowest income, so expanding bus service (especially when in conjunction with more open housing policies) could help to reduce economic segregation.

To elaborate on the logic of transportation systems as catalysts and filters, I employ the vocabulary of network analysis in developing a verbal theory of infrastructure-induced sorting. We can think of communities to which households might migrate as a set of *nodes* connected by transportation lines, or *edges*. While the insights could apply to infrastructure-induced migration between any set of communities connected by an infrastructure network, they are especially pertinent to highways' influence on residential sorting.

Increasing capacity of an open-access transportation network can facilitate (catalyze) sorting by reducing the costs of commuting to and from a new neighborhood. As travel costs between nodes decrease (such as through improved transportation technology or infrastructure), households can maintain their previous utility while acting on their preferences for the goods provided in specific communities accessible via the new transportation infrastructure (Tiebout, 1956). Work in regional economics has supported this way of modeling residential choice, showing how exogenous changes in mobility may affect residential trade-offs. Yamada (1972), for example, shows that households make trade-offs between "accessibility and space," "space and leisure," and "accessibility and travel time" (125). The introduction of a "new technique" for increasing travel speeds (for example, a major expressway) need not result in more leisure or work time (as one might expect). Instead, households may choose to take residence in locations farther from their workplaces to enjoy more affordable real estate or place-based amenities (such as open space) not accessible under the previous transportation system (135).[6] This has implications for partisan residential sorting and segregation, as well. Instead of pocketing the additional disposable time made available by transportation infrastructure, partisans may use their commuting-time surplus to choose communities compatible with a range of other preferences. These preferences may be associated with their partisanship (Tiebout, 1956).[7]

Transportation infrastructure's implications for sorting depend on households' ability to act on their preferences within their time and resource constraints. However, these preferences are often externally constrained by local policies that restrict housing options. *Where discriminatory or economically exclusionary housing practices exist, improved transportation infrastructure can exacerbate segregation by expanding residential options only among those allowed to migrate to take residence in communities.* Improved transportation networks increase mobility for everyone with access to the transportation mode, and this can be of general benefit regardless of local housing practices. However, when communities discriminate on correlates of partisanship, including income and race, increased mobility may increase partisan segregation. For example, as the federal highway program facilitated suburban development, growing communities along new highways engaged in racial discrimination by adopting restrictive zoning practices, racial deed restrictions, or more direct resistance.[8] Today, a primary instrument by which discrimination occurs is through restrictive land-use rules (or "downzoning"), through R1 zoning (which limits development to single-family homes), minimum lot-size requirements, and other local development restrictions (Levine, 2006; Fischel, 2015). By prohibiting or greatly restricting multiunit rental housing in a municipality, such zoning is, on average, more likely to exclude Democrats: across the years of the General Social Survey (1972–2014), 71 percent of Republican respondents but only 60 percent of self-identified Democrats owned their own homes (Smith, Marsden, and Hout, 2015).[9]

Finally, transportation infrastructure can act as a filter, facilitating sorting through racial and socioeconomic differences in access to, and use of, specific transportation infrastructure. Travel costs vary by transportation mode, resulting selection of modal user groups with different partisan compositions. Holding all else equal, the partisan composition of communities will tend to reflect the partisanship of users of the transportation systems that serve the community. For example, at one extreme, city buses primarily serve low-income riders. Holding all else equal and absent housing restrictions, expanded bus service will allow the car-less poor to extend the geographic scope of their job and housing opportunities. Interstate highways, on the other hand, disproportionately deliver their benefits to those who drive their own cars, increasing the commuting options of a larger but relatively more affluent group. Even some forms of mass transit may introduce filtering effects, particularly when they are too costly for the poor. Commuter and intercity rail systems, for example, attract users with higher incomes and sometimes charge substantial fares that effectively exclude lower-income travelers.[10] For example, individuals with incomes over \$75,000 per year account for 56 percent of the peak-hour uses of commuter rail but only 18 percent of the peak-hour bus and light rail users (Pucher and Renne, 2003, 18). Moreover, this filtering results partisan differences in the respective user bases of the different mass transit modes. In a multiyear transportation survey conducted by the Mineta Transportation Institute at San José State University, 30 percent of self-reported registered Democrats but only 15 percent of registered Republicans reported using transit in the previous month.[11]

The American Highway Network as Catalyst and Filter

By delivering an exogenous positive shock to travel speeds, federally financed highways acted as both catalyst and filter for partisan residential sorting. In an original survey on partisan residential preferences, I show that increased travel speeds allow individuals to select into communities on the basis of preferences either explicitly driven by or correlated with their partisanship. I also present qualitative evidence related to the other aspect of the catalyst effect: highways have facilitated specific types of exclusionary development. A survey of newspaper advertisements from the 1960s and 1970s reveals that real estate developers explicitly linked the convenience of suburban highways and the advantages of exclusionary, "restricted" suburban communities. Finally, data from the 1963 Census of Transportation, released in the earliest years of the Interstate Highway System, provide evidence supporting the filter effect. In the early 1960s, automobile commuters were more likely to have professional occupations and to live longer distances from their work, and would reap benefits from the Interstate Highway System.

Interstate Highways Reduced Americans' Daily Travel Costs

Highways are consequential because even modest increases in travel speeds can change the residential choice calculus of commuting-averse Americans. Avoidance of long commutes has been a persistent behavioral feature of the American commuter. In the 1963 Census of Transportation, only 9 percent of Americans reported spending 30 minutes or more on their one-way work commutes (United States. Department of Commerce. Bureau of the Census, 1966, 72). Americans are now more likely to have long daily commutes, but their behavior indicates that they still avoid long commuting times: fewer than 10 percent of American workers spend more than 60 minutes on one-way commutes and 47 percent have one-way commutes of under 20 minutes (Pisarski, 2006, 102).

Understanding that Americans rarely tolerate long commutes, we can infer how highway-induced improvements in travel speeds (especially in the post-Interstate era) facilitated residential sorting. While it is accepted that the Interstate program greatly increased travel speeds, changes in speeds only appear in scattered public records. Historical, locally specific travel-speed data are difficult to obtain, except from local case studies and road maps displaying intercity travel times. Analyses based on these sources show that the Interstate Highway System greatly expanded Americans' plausible daily driving range. In 1964, the industry-affiliated Automotive Safety Foundation published a publicity booklet, *What Freeways Mean to Your City*, pointing to an Eno Transportation Foundation study of the Los Angeles freeway system (Automotive Safety Foundation, 1964). The study concluded that new freeways cut rush-hour travel times in that city by 40–50 percent in the years immediately following highway construction. Another study found that expansion of Interstate highways in the Kansas City metropolitan area quintupled the area reachable by an hour's drive from downtown (Pucher, 1998). Of course, expansion of daily commuting range did not occur only between downtowns and suburbs. Similar improvements in driving speeds occurred along "outer belt" highways connecting suburban cities as well, facilitating the growth of so-called "edge cities" (Garreau, 1991).

Most historical evidence on highways' effects on travel speeds has come from scattered sources. To analyze the effects of new highways on travel speed more comprehensively, I collected historical data from Rand McNally road atlases published before and after construction of the Interstate Highway System. Beginning in 1952, Rand McNally began producing its "Map of the United States Featuring Transcontinental Mileage and Driving Time," a map-style network diagram that has appeared in all subsequent atlases. These diagrams report the total mileage and travel time between major cities and junctions, accounting for "topography, speed laws, and congested areas" (Rand McNally and Company, 1952, 106).

To use these diagrams to capture changes in intercity travel speeds to and from each city over time, I calculated the cumulative miles reported on all road network segments emanating from each city and divided the result by the cumulative driving times reported on the segments.[12] As shown in Figure 2.1, in 1952, travel on routes emanating from major cities and connecting nearby junctions and cities averaged only 36 miles per hour. By 1975, after completion of almost all Interstate mileage, average intercity speeds had increased to 45 miles per hour.[13] The resulting implications for metropolitan areas have been far greater than one might expect from a single-digit change in travel speeds. For example, in a hypothetical circular metropolitan area with a 36-mile-per-hour average highway speed on routes emanating radially from a city's central business district, a commuter would have 1,017 square miles over which to choose a place of residence.[14] Increasing average speeds to 45 miles per hour increases that zone by one-and-a-half times, to 1,590 square miles, adding an area as large as Phoenix, Arizona.[15]

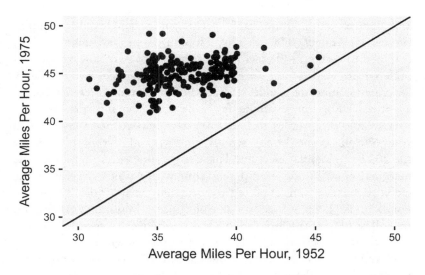

Figure 2.1. Average travel speeds on routes emanating from cities and junctions in 1952 (before construction of most Interstates under the Federal Aid Highway Act of 1956) and in 1975, after completion of most Interstate highway construction. Source: *Rand McNally Road Atlas*, 1952 and 1975.

The Catalyst Effect: Facilitating Sorting Under Homophily

It is one thing to show that highways facilitated suburbanization by expanding the geographic extent of the average American's residential and employment options. But to show that highways were ultimately responsible for catalyzing *partisan* sorting, we must establish that Democrats and Republicans differed in their residential preferences while also being responsive to daily driving time. On the first point, survey evidence has been extensive. Roper and Gallup surveys conducted in the 1970s and 1980s, as well as more recent surveys on partisan polarization, show Republicans as anywhere from 10 to 20 points less likely than Democrats to prefer living in cities or urbanized areas (e.g., Roper Organization, 1976; Gallup Organization, 1983; Pew Research Center, 2014). However, such survey items have usually asked respondents to describe their ideal living arrangements without requiring them to address their resource constraints or to account for the practical trade-offs required by their residential choices.

To examine how Americans cope with such trade-offs, Jonathan Mummolo and I conducted a survey of 4,800 self-identified Democrats and Republicans in June 2013.[16] This survey employed a conjoint survey experiment (Hainmueller, Hopkins, and Yamamoto, 2014) designed to ascertain the factors contributing to partisans' residential preferences. Respondents were asked to choose between two randomly generated composite profiles of hypothetical communities (zip codes) as displayed in the example in Table 2.1. The information used to assemble the profiles included urban–suburban place type, racial composition, crime levels, school quality, and two-party vote in the 2012 presidential election. This design allowed estimation of the marginal contribution of different community traits. Several of the included factors were expected to yield few partisan disagreements. For example, housing cost is a driving concern in residential selection regardless of partisanship, and this was randomized across three levels: 15 percent, 25 percent, and 40 percent of respondent pretax income. The crime rate was set to two values, arbitrarily selected to provide a relative sense of the local crime level: 20 percent above the national average or 20 percent below the national average.[17] "School quality score" was reported on a ten-point scale similar to those that appear

Table 2.1. *Example from the conjoint comparison exercise used in Mummolo and Nall (2017). Respondents viewed and chose communities from nine similar randomly generated pairs.*

Community Trait	Community A	Community B
Total daily driving time for commuting and errands	25 min	45 min
Type of place	Suburban neighborhood with mix of shops, houses, and businesses	Small town
Housing cost	15 percent of pretax income	30 percent of pretax income
Race	90% white, 10% nonwhite	50% white, 50% nonwhite
Violent crime rate (vs national rate)	20% more crime than national average	20% less crime than national average
Presidential vote in 2012	30% Democrat, 70% Republican	70% Democrat, 30% Republican
School quality rating (1=worst, 10=best)	9	9

on real estate search sites, taking a value of 5 (middling school quality) or 9 (very high school quality). Other categories on the survey were expected to yield larger partisan differences. "Type of place" took on one of six levels used in other residential preference surveys: city downtown with a mix of shops, businesses, and homes; city residential area; mixed-use suburban neighborhood; suburban neighborhood with houses only; small town; and rural area (Belden, Russonello, and Stewart, 2011). A community's racial composition was expressed in terms of the white/nonwhite racial composition of the neighborhood, randomized across four levels: 50 percent white/50 percent nonwhite, 75 percent white/25 percent nonwhite, 90 percent white/10 percent nonwhite, or 96 percent white/4 percent nonwhite. Finally, a hypothetical community's partisan composition was expressed in terms of the 2012 presidential vote, randomized across three levels: 30 percent Democratic/70 percent Republican, 50 percent Democratic/50 percent Republican, and 70 percent Democrat/30 percent Republican. Any combination of levels for each of the preceding traits could have appeared in each profile included in each pair.

Respondents expressed their choices over nine different profile pairs.[18] Data from this exercise were analyzed using a linear probability model to estimate Democrats' and Republicans' preference for a community given a set of listed traits.[19] Full results of this exercise for both parties are reported in Figure 2.2. These results show that Democrats and Republicans respond in the same ways to certain "valence" attributes (such as housing costs and crime levels) but diverge substantially over urban versus rural type of place and other neighborhood social and political traits. After accounting for other included factors, both Democrats and Republicans were 8 points more likely to prefer a politically balanced community over one dominated by the other party. However, such stated preferences over neighborhood partisanship are unnecessary for partisan sorting to occur. Partisan differences over community-level correlates of community partisan composition may also lead to partisan sorting. One of those correlates is race. When asked to choose between a 50 percent nonwhite community and comparison communities with larger white populations, Republicans were 12 points more likely to choose a 96 percent white community, holding all else equal, while Democrats (mostly as a result of their more diverse personal racial identification) preferred more racially diverse communities.[20]

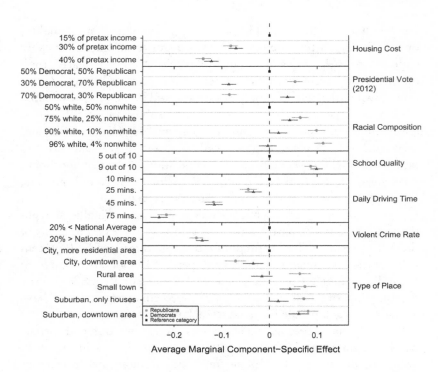

Figure 2.2. Average marginal component-specific effects of community traits on residential selection among self-identified Democrats and Republicans. Members of the two parties agree on community quality, but disagree over racial and political composition and urban versus rural character.

Democrats and Republicans have in common an aversion to additional driving time that substantially dictates their stated residential preferences. While partisan respondents diverged over urban versus rural character, racial composition, and partisan composition (Figure 2.2), they reacted negatively to additional driving time. Both Democrats and Republicans were 12 percentage points more likely to prefer living in a community requiring 10 minutes of daily driving time than one requiring 45 minutes. Increasing commuting time by an additional 30 minutes reduced the probability of neighborhood selection by an additional 10–12 points for members of both parties. To put this in perspective, a 35 minute increase in commuting time had the same negative effect on stated residential preference as increasing the violent crime rate (from 20 percent below to 20 percent above the national average), cutting the school quality rating from a 9 to a 5, or increasing a person's housing cost from 15 percent to 40 percent of annual income.

Highway improvements can deliver additional time to commuters, which they may use to commute greater distances. We might expect them to use this time to choose more politically compatible communities. To demonstrate this, I estimated additional linear probability models, interacting the total daily driving time variable with each of the other variables and reporting the average probability that Democrats and Republicans selected a community under combinations of travel time and community traits. These analyses indicate that improvements in travel speeds enable Democrats and Republicans to act on their different residential preferences while maintaining their overall utility.

Figure 2.3 presents respondents' predicted utility (the probability a community was selected) as a function of daily drive time and other community characteristics.[21] In each of these graphs, the intersections of a horizontal line and the curves drawn across the graphs indicate the levels of the two variables (driving time and the other community characteristic) at which an average respondent would be indifferent between two communities. These relationships are reported for Republicans and Democrats in interaction plots showing the predicted probability a community was selected at daily driving times of 10, 25, 45, and 75 minutes per day, across levels of the other variable. The graphs in Figure 2.3 display trade-offs between driving time and the three factors on which Democrats and Republicans disagreed: type of place, racial composition, and partisan composition. The analysis shows that improved highways are likely to allow households to choose from more politically compatible neighborhoods while maintaining their utility levels. Higher speeds may be used to shorten commutes, delivering additional utility that offset undesirable features of neighborhoods, or they may increase utility by enabling partisans to capture the benefits of access to additional, more desirable neighborhoods while maintaining the same daily driving times.

As these graphs indicate, Republicans, who state a preference for more homogeneously white, less urban, and more Republican communities, may be more able to act on these concerns with the additional mobility provided by express highways, while mobility enhancements may be less likely to facilitate sorting by Democrats.

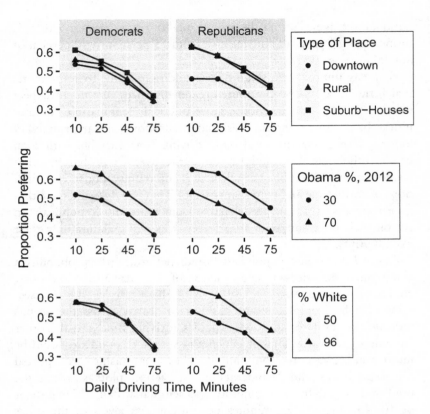

Figure 2.3. Probabilities that Democrats and Republicans select a community, as a function of daily driving time and polarizing community traits. Any horizontal line across the graph intersects with combinations of driving time and community-characteristic level that would result in equal utility.

The left column of Figure 2.3 shows how Republicans' utility varies by commuting time and traits that are typically associated with partisanship. Republicans would, on average, choose any nonurban place over a downtown one, even if living downtown spared them from daily driving entirely. They are, on average, generally indifferent between communities that are predominantly white (e.g., 96 percent white versus 90 percent white). However, the results suggest that they would be willing to endure substantial daily commuting hardship to avoid the most racially diverse communities. For example, based on the utilities estimated here, a Republican would increase her commute from 25 minutes to 75 minutes per day to live in a community that is 96 percent versus 50 percent white. The same types of trade-offs arise with respect to partisan composition's limited direct contribution to neighborhood evaluations. Mummolo and Nall (2017) show that the partisan composition of a community does not usually rate highly on a list of concerns. However, Americans may use partisanship as a proxy for other community traits, ranging from their neighbors' attitudes toward taxation to cosmopolitanism and cultural preferences (Hui, 2013; Gimpel and Hui, 2015).

The right column of Figure 2.3 shows that Democrats are also likely to react to improvements in driving speeds, though the pairwise trade-offs that they are likely to make among driving time and other relevant community traits – urbanism, racial diversity, and partisan composition – are weaker. Democrats, for example, are more indifferent than Republicans to community racial composition (across most levels of diversity), so changes in driving time are less relevant to Democrats' responses on that dimension. Similarly, their response to urban places is less consistently negative than Republicans'. However, Democrats, like Republicans, state a preference for living among copartisans, and an exogenous reduction in travel times might facilitate residential choices in response to that preference. (Of course, like Republicans, they may use community partisanship as a proxy for other community traits.)

For both Democrats and Republicans, the value of increasing travel speeds is not just in the direct improvement in utility, but in the expansion of residential options that satisfy their preferences while maintaining the same daily travel burdens.

The Catalyst Effect: Exacerbating the Effect of Discriminatory Practices

An additional way that highways catalyze sorting is by exacerbating the effects of discriminatory and exclusionary real estate practices. The federal highway program, and especially the Interstate Highway System, opened millions of acres to residential development, often in rural and suburban municipalities with restrictive zoning policies. The postwar Interstate program offered real estate developers and agents immense opportunities to develop suburban housing. In a 1964 report on the social and economic effects of highways, the Bureau of Public

Roads reported that the Interstate Highway System would expose to residential development anywhere from 3.73 to 7.46 million acres (United States. Department of Commerce. Bureau of Public Roads, 1964), 13.

Real estate developers capitalized on this spatial expansion by building new suburban housing tracts.[22] While real estate entrepreneurs engaged in discriminatory practices in cities (Massey and Denton, 1993, 37), they were working at the destination of "white flight" as well. In the suburbs, they built new housing developments tailored to a preferred set of residents.[23]

In marketing suburban housing, real estate marketers capitalized on the sentiments motivating white flight, blending messages about cities' shortcomings with complementary messages about the suburban advantages that were now more accessible via modern express highways. Newspaper real estate advertisements from the 1960s and 1970s reveal that marketers were attentive to the ways new transportation infrastructure would make suburbs more accessible and appealing to their target audience. Moreover, developers revealed an understanding of expressways' contribution to exclusionary housing development practices. To study how real estate developers reacted to new highway developments, I collected newspaper advertisements from the Sunday real estate sections of five major newspapers: the *New York Times, Washington Post, St. Louis Post-Dispatch, Atlanta Journal*, and *Houston Chronicle*, focusing on spring real estate sections from March and April, collected at five-year intervals froim 1960 to 1975. Research assistants identified advertisements that mentioned local highways as an important advantage of the real estate offering.[24]

While advertisements for new residential developments rarely mentioned highways as an important amenity (focusing instead on the advertised properties themselves), the advertising search identified many cases in which real estate promoters noted that their development's location on a major highway would allow residents to maintain access to the central city while reaping the advantages of suburbia.[25] In addition to advertising the particular private benefits provided to home buyers, advertisements discussed the local mixture of public goods and taxes, as well as the neighborhood's accessibility to regional commercial centers and destinations.

Some advertisements discussed highways' role as a catalyst of suburban exclusion in surprisingly explicit terms. For example, a 1965 advertisement for Sherwood, a single-family residential development in the Houston exurb of Pearland, Texas announced that it was "only 20 minutes from Houston" on the Gulf Freeway, and listed a range of amenities described in lightly coded language sure to appeal to mid-1960s conservatives: "a highly *restricted* [emphasis added] neighborhood ... all home sites are extra large ... 24-hour police and fire protection ... top ranking schools ... lower taxes."[26] Another advertisement from this period, for another Gulf Freeway community called Sagemont, advertised that it would be a "carefully planned community with the highest restrictions," and would have "its own schools, churches, and shopping facilities."[27] An advertisement in the March 13, 1965, issue of the *Atlanta Journal* promoted a new Marietta neighborhood called "Stratford," located adjacent to Atlanta's Perimeter Road outer loop highway and billed as "Metropolitan Atlanta's escape from noise, tension, and social unrest."[28] Given what we know about the scope of racially and economically exclusionary real estate practices in the postwar era, these ads help highlight how a federal highway program, mostly implemented without discriminatory intent, facilitated white flight and exclusionary housing.[29]

The Filter Effect

Highways themselves can also more directly drive partisan geographic sorting. Of course, highways disproportionately benefit Americans who own or have access to automobiles. Even when carless Americans do have access to a car, it is not always feasible – as a result of scarce time and financial resources – for poorer Americans to regularly drive the distances that must be covered by suburban expressway commuters. This fact has been the basis of scholarship on spatial mismatch: that the immobile poor find themselves living in neighborhoods that lack access to jobs (Kain, 1968; Wilson, 1987). An implication of the existing socioeconomic distribution of automobile and transit users is that new highway infrastructure will, all else equal, expand job and housing options only for those with the resources to use the new highways.[30] Low-SES workers have long been less likely than high-SES workers to use automobiles, or to commute long distances in their personal automobiles, meaning that high-SES workers have been able to live farther from work and enjoy more residential options. For example, in 1963, during the earliest years of the Interstate era, white-collar professionals were twice as likely as service workers to live 11 or more miles from work (26 percent versus 13 percent), and less likely than service workers to live within 3 miles of their jobs (25 percent versus 36 percent). Despite living farther from work on average, a larger proportion of high-status workers enjoyed short commutes of under 15 minutes (29 percent versus 25 percent), and fewer of the high-status workers had commutes longer than 35 minutes (15 percent versus 18 percent) (United States. Department of Commerce. Bureau of the Census, 1966, 75). In short, high-status commuters have rarely been confined to neighborhoods near their place of work. They have long been more likely than low-status workers to drive their own cars to work, and less likely to walk, bike, or use transit. Even in 1963, when transit usage was still coming off its wartime peak (Jones, 2008), professional workers were only about a third as likely as domestic workers to use public transit to get to work (9 percent versus 24 percent), and were one and a half times as likely to drive to work in a personal automobile (68 percent versus 42 percent) (United States. Department of Commerce. Bureau of the Census, 1966, 76).[31]

Even as transportation infrastructure has improved, the relative socioeconomic distribution of highway and transit users has changed little since the 1960s. The National Household Travel Survey of 2001 (Pucher and Renne, 2003) indicates that highways are likely to continue acting as a filter. While automobile commuters are on average middle class, highways can still facilitate socioeconomic sorting by excluding Americans who lack automobile access. Contrary to conventional wisdom, even users of different transit programs vary economically, sometimes substantially. Figure 2.4 plots the proportion of peak-hour transportation mode users with incomes below $20,000 per year and greater than $100,000 per year. Some 37 percent of bus and light rail users were low income and only 8 percent were high income. At the opposite extreme, commuter rail lines serve a wealthier clientele (42 percent high – income, only 3 percent low – income). What this means is that some forms of transit lines, such as light rail or buses, may reduce inequality and possibly reduce residential segregation by expanding residential and job options for the poor, while commuter rail lines that connect central business districts and

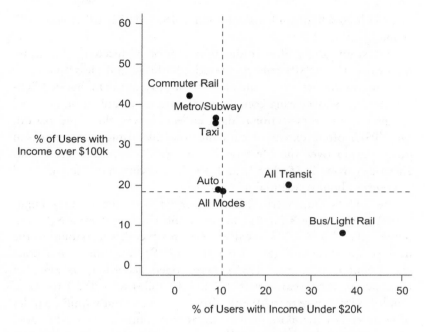

Figure 2.4. Percentage of peak-hour commuters in high and low income categories, by transportation mode. The horizontal and vertical dashed lines indicate the average for all transportation modes for each income group. Source: Pucher and Renne (2003, 18).

affluent suburban communities (e.g., New Jersey Transit, the Long Island Railroad, the San Francisco Peninsula Caltrain) and exclude low-income riders may facilitate residential options for their affluent rider base.[32] However, the bus and light rail modes that dominate transit in most metropolitan areas are more likely to facilitate the mobility of the poor, possibly expanding their residential options.

Evidence from Historical Panel Survey Data

Is Americans' moving behavior consistent with the mechanism outlined in the preceding sections? Few individual-level or household-level data are available that would allow us to track behavior over the full postwar period. A fortunate exception is the Youth-Parent Socialization Panel Study (YPSPS), a unique survey panel of 935 Class of 1965 high school students collected in 1965, 1973, 1982, and 1997 (Jennings et al., 2005).

This study allows for study of migration induced by Interstate highways. The YPSPS cohort entered adulthood and chose places of residence in the late 1960s and early 1970s, just as the Interstate Highway System was nearing completion. In addition, unlike other panel or time-series cross-sectional data collected over the same period, the YPSPS offers extensive data on political attitudes and partisan identification over the life course. The YPSPS includes respondent zip codes from 1965, 1982, and 1997, allowing more fine-grained inferences about residential migration.[33]

The YPSPS data were spatially merged with the Federal Highway Administration's PR-511 highway construction database (Baum-Snow, 2007*a*) in ArcGIS to calculate each zip code's proximity to the nearest Interstate and nearest major city.[34] Self-identified Democrats and Republicans (as of 1997) were coded according to place of residence in each year: urban (within 10 miles of a 1950 top-one-hundred city), more than 10 miles from such a city but within 10 miles of an Interstate, or more than 10 miles from both a top-one-hundred city and an Interstate highway.[35]

The least squares regression models presented in Table 2.2 reveal that Republicans were much more likely than Democrats to move to suburbs along Interstate highways between 1965 and 1997. I present linear models estimating the probability that partisan respondents starting in specific locations migrated into suburbs along Interstate highways across the time period. While it is difficult to infer individual motives from self-reported migration data alone, information from the conjoint analysis suggests that Americans likely migrated in response to correlates of partisanship, such as the racial and ethnic and economic composition of communities and their urban–rural location.

Table 2.2 reports least squares estimates of urban high school graduates' migration to Interstate suburbs. Model 1 is a simple regression of residence in an Interstate suburb against a three-category party variable for Democratic, Independent, and Republican identifiers as of 1997. The next two columns are also simple regressions, one using only *White* race (Model 2) as a predictor, the other using a three-category variable for *Annual family income in 1973* (Model 3).[36] Model 4 includes party, race, and income variables. Models 5 through

Table 2.2. *Least squares regression of socioeconomic, racial, and political predictors of migration to Interstate suburbs by 1956 high-school graduates. Data: Jennings et al. (2005).*

	Urban H.S. Grads (1965)				Non urban H.S. Grads (1965)			
	(1)	(2)	(3)	(4)	(5)	(6)	(7)	(8)
(Intercept)	0.33*	0.19*	0.37*	0.15	0.44*	0.53*	0.39*	0.43
	(0.11)	(0.08)	(0.09)	(0.12)	(0.04)	(0.08)	(0.06)	(0.10)
Party: I	0.11			0.07	0.03			0.04
	(0.07)			(0.08)	(0.10)			(0.06)
Party: R	0.16*			0.11	0.10*			0.11*
	(0.08)			(0.08)	(0.05)			(0.05)
White Race		0.26*		0.22*		−0.05		−0.10
		(0.09)		(0.10)		(0.08)		(0.09)
Mid. Inc. (1973)			0.04	0.01			0.04	0.09
			(0.11)	(0.10)			(0.10)	(0.06)
High Inc. (1973)			0.05	0.03			0.05	0.16*
			(0.11)	(0.10)			(0.11)	(0.07)
N	266	266	266	266	658	658	658	658

Standard errors in parentheses, calculated using method in Rubin (1987).
* Indicates significance at $p < 0.05$.
Reported N is average of subsets from the five multiply imputed data sets.

8 feature the same predictors as Models 1 through 4, but for graduates of nonurban high schools.[37]

These models are not intended to identify Interstate highways' causal effect on residential location. However, the models do reveal individual migration behavior consistent with the catalyst-filter mechanisms described earlier in the chapter. They confirm that Republicans and groups likely to become Republican were more likely to move into suburbs along Interstates than other groups. "White flight" appears to be one mechanism by which this partisan migration occurred. Urban high school graduates who identified as Republicans as of 1997 were 16 points more likely than self-identified Democrats to live in suburban or rural zip codes along Interstates. As reported in Model 2, white graduates of urban high schools were 26 points more likely than nonwhites to move from the central city to an Interstate suburb. Point estimates for each of the income categories (Model 3) were in the expected direction but imprecisely estimated, suggesting that income sorting was likely less pivotal than sorting on factors tied to race or party. In Model 4, which includes race, income, and party terms, only the coefficient on white race is statistically significant, though the coefficient estimate on party continues to be in the expected direction. Of course, racial identification and partisanship are sufficiently related that disentangling them can be difficult, but the implications for partisan residential sorting are clear and substantively significant.

Graduates of nonurban high schools also migrated into communities along Interstate highways. Republicans from nonurban high schools were 10 points more likely than Democrats to be living in an Interstate suburb by 1997 (Model 5), but neither white race nor income were significant predictors of residence in a suburb near Interstates (Models 6 and 7). In total, these results indicate two major, and perhaps tightly connected, mechanisms by which Interstates led to partisan geographic sorting along highways. Republicans were more likely than Democrats to migrate to suburban and rural areas along Interstate highways, and this shift occurred concurrently with white flight and economic segregation.

As the YPSPS results suggest, partisan sorting may happen in two ways: geographic movement of existing partisans, or party-switching of existing residents, either in place or some time after moving to a new location and changing their partisanship. Ongoing secular realignments, such as the shift of Southern whites out of the

Democratic Party, are important to this account. While addressing this specific mechanism may be of great importance to scholars attempting to isolate the suburbs' contextual effects, it is not as important in assessing highways' aggregate influence on political geography. Nevertheless, the results presented here – and especially multifaceted evidence on the importance of white flight and new suburban growth – all point to present-day partisan geographic polarization being, at least in part, the result of migration of voters who were already Republican or likely to become Republican. While postmigration contextual effects may have driven some of the resulting suburban partisan change (Gainsborough, 2001), the arrival of new voters with more conservative and antiurban preferences has been central to suburban Republican growth. Highways have been a critical contributor to that growth.

Conclusion

Highways have been central to the expansion and political development of metropolitan areas. They have made possible sorting on many dimensions, including partisanship. At least since the mid-1970s, Democrats and Republicans have both stated and expressed different residential preferences. Partisan differences are not primarily a result of express preferences to live in co-partisan communities, but also reflects interparty differences over communities' racial, economic, and urban characteristics (Roper Organization, 1976; Gallup Organization, 1983; Belden, Russonello, and Stewart, 2011; Pew Research Center, 2014; Mummolo and Nall, 2017). Yet this chapter has shown that such preferences are meaningless if Americans do not have the means to act on them. To a considerable degree, highways have been that means. Without them racial, economic, and partisan sorting would not have occurred on such a large geographic scale in the post-Interstate era. Moreover, While nothing about highways is inherently discriminatory, they have facilitated household-level sorting decisions in the context of both individual-level homophily and local discriminatory practices. In the next chapter, I present additional historical geographical data that support this account: the Interstate highway program made fast-growing suburban counties more Republican than they would have been otherwise, and they added to urban–suburban polarization in leading metropolitan areas.

Notes

1 To borrow from Anatole France, much as the law in its majestic equality forbids the rich and poor alike to sleep under bridges and steal bread, the American highway system in its equality provided the means for rich and poor, black and white with automobiles to access housing and commute by car to jobs throughout metropolitan areas.

2 For a recent review of this extensive literature in the context of racial segregation, see Oliver (2010), pp. 101–3.

3 Schelling (1971*a*) is often misinterpreted and used as a strawman in racial segregation scholarship. Schelling (1971*a*) acknowledges that, in practice, other factors, including "organized discrimination" (especially racial) or the "economically induced" segregation resulting from inequality in economic relationships, could be more important than individual-level household preferences for specific types of neighbors (Schelling, 1971*a*, 144).

4 Warner (1978) showed how streetcar lines in the Boston area facilitated development of working-class and middle-class housing in "streetcar suburbs." Such fixed-route transportation lines tended to attract high-density housing occupied by citizens who did not own automobiles. Other scholars, building on a long tradition in urban economics, show how changing transportation systems influence urban form (Kain, 1962; Alonso, 1964; Mieszkowski and Mills, 1993). For example, when automobiles were a luxury item, lower socioeconomic classes were forced to live within walking distance to work or transit lines. During the streetcar age, the only economically viable place to build apartment complexes was along transit lines (Fischel, 2015, 182–4). While these accounts have highlighted transportation's influence on urban form, they rarely account for the role transportation networks have played in emerging political geography. However, see Rodden (2014), who examines railroads' influence on the location of industrial housing and the concentration of left parties in central cities.

5 In the simplest case, one could regard this as a standard Schelling sorting model, but accounting for travel costs.

6 Choosing to accept long commutes in exchange for better local amenities at one's home is not a phenomenon exclusive to suburbanization. For example, young professionals often opt to live in central cities and "reverse commute" to jobs in suburban office parks. See Kain (1962).

7 People need not consciously associate their preferences with partisanship for partisan sorting to result. Mummolo and Nall (2017) distinguish between homophily (the general tendency of socially similar persons to cluster geographically, sometimes consciously) and partisan discrimination (people actively incorporating politics into

their moving decisions). Intentions are less important than revealed preferences.

8 See, for example, Sugrue's 1995 account of Detroit whites' resistance to residential integration. For more extended accounts of exclusionary housing practices, see Fogelson (2005) and Trounstine (2016).

9 While racial discrimination by landlords and real estate agents is prohibited under the Fair Housing Act of 1968, the law does nothing to address the disparate impact of zoning. Such land-use restrictions have effectively impeded implementation of two federal policies that subsidize private housing markets to assist low-income households: the Low-Income Housing Tax Credit, which provides tax benefits to developers who build housing with low-income units, and Section 8 vouchers, which directly subsidize low-income beneficiaries' rent payments (United States. Congressional Budget Office, 2015).

10 The Main Line suburbs of Philadelphia, which grew around the nation's first commuter rail line, are one example (Stilgoe, 1985). More current examples can be found in present-day transit systems. For example, on the Bay Area's suburban BART Yellow Line, a round trip from the remote suburb of Pittsburg to downtown San Francisco was $13.10 in April 2016, the equivalent of about an hour's pay even under the generous minimum wage in the region.

11 See Agrawal, Nixon, and Nall (2017) for a discussion of the partisan results. For individual survey reports, see Agrawal and Nixon (2011a, b); Agrawal, Nixon, and Murthy (2012); Agrawal and Nixon (2013, 2014, 2015).

12 Across this time period, junctions were sometimes removed excluded from the Rand McNally maps when primary routes between cities changed.

13 The travel speeds reported in 1975 also have much lower variance, suggesting that Interstate highways standardized intercity travel speeds throughout the country.

14 This simplified account assumes that drivers might be able to exploit this increase in travel speeds in any radial direction from the city center.

15 To keep the illustration simple, this hypothetical is based on a monocentric model with a single urban employment center. In practice, jobs are usually located in the suburbs, providing a multiplicity of employment and housing choices that also increase with highway improvements.

16 For full details on the methods and data used in the conjoint study, see Mummolo and Nall (2017).

17 Since survey respondents usually have little direct understanding or knowledge of statistics such as the actual national crime rate (or even their local crime rate), this approach was meant to be a compromise

between merely offering subjective categories ("safe" and "unsafe") versus giving people a fixed reference point against which they might evaluate a community.

18 To be sure, some trait combinations (for example, certain racial and urbanism measures) are improbable and nearly unrealistic. Testing this using precinct data from 2008 as a real-world measure of partisanship, and American Community Survey data on zip-code tabulation area (ZCTA) demographics, the 450 zip codes in the United States that were 70 percent (69.5 percent to 70.5 percent) Republican were, on average, 89 percent white, but one of the zip codes was only 35 percent white. We deliberately constructed the conjoint profiles to minimize the number of unrealistic community profiles.

19 The residential choice was expressed as a binary dependent variable and attribute levels enter into the regression as categorical variables (omitting a reference category for each). The coefficient on each attribute level thus represents its effect on the respondent's probability of selecting a community, after controlling for combinations of other traits (Hainmueller, Hopkins, and Yamamoto, 2014, 11). Specifically, these coefficients are estimated by combining the $J \cdot K$ choices for each respondent into a panel data set. The outcome variable, Y_{jk}, is coded 1 if the community described in profile jk was selected, and zero otherwise. The explanatory variables included in each row were the randomized values of the L categorical variables used as traits for each community option jk. A least squares regression model with standard errors clustered by respondent (Arai, 2011) was applied to these data.

20 At least when it comes to stated preferences, white and nonwhite Democrats derived less marginal utility from homogeneously white communities than Republicans did. The composite profiles used in the conjoint design allowed individuals to conceal their underlying motivations for any particular choice. Only by giving each individual an impractically large number of conjoint choice exercises would it be possible to determine their individual responses to a community's racial composition.

21 The fully randomized conjoint design allows for unbiased effect estimates for any combination of terms included in the profiles (Hainmueller, Hopkins, and Yamamoto, 2014).

22 Real estate developers and agents, who facilitated exclusionary housing practices across the twentieth century, have long engaged in land speculation around new transportation infrastructure networks. Even before the construction of Interstates, real estate developers and speculators tied their fortunes to local transportation infrastructure. Railroads and streetcars once stimulated local residential development (Warner, 1978),

but by the early twentieth century highways were facilitating growth in areas far removed from rail lines (Hawley, 1956, 13). "Arterial" roads, whether early boulevards or major non-Interstate highways, became the axes around which new homes, commercial businesses, and industrial plants were built (Jackson, 1985, 165). In Detroit, for example, an early paved thoroughfare, Woodward Avenue, which expanded to eight lanes by the 1920s, was marketed as a major local amenity by realtors selling homes along the route. Real estate developers facilitated their suburban home sales by appealing to, and capitalizing on, the development of the new roads.

23 For more discussion on the history of discriminatory policies in the suburbs, see Trounstine (2016).

24 Research assistants only recorded ads for real estate developments. The search excluded classified ads for individual home sites.

25 The search also yielded evidence of developers' response to ephemeral changes in residential preferences. For example, advertisements in 1975, in the energy-conscious era after the 1973 OPEC oil embargo crisis, mentioned energy efficiency and walkability, but this selling point decreased in frequency as the crisis faded.

26 *Houston Chronicle*, April 4, 1965, pp. 11–6.

27 *Houston Chronicle*, March 14, 1965, pp. 10–10.

28 *Atlanta Journal*, March 13, 1965, p. 16C.

29 On the question of discriminatory intent, Rothstein (2017) shows that some highway proponents believed that highways would facilitate urban renewal. Rothstein alleges that highways were deliberately used to facilitate racial segregation (127–31). A remaining open question is the extent to which highways interacted with the development of local housing regulations. Due to the American tradition of local home rule in housing regulation, we have hardly any machine-readable data on present-day local policies controlling housing, let alone historical data. As the Sunlight Foundation notes, even with adoption of new technologies that allow sharing of housing rules, municipalities impede access to such data by publishing it in non-machine-readable forms such as PDF tables and maps (Green, 2013). Even when data on public land-use regulation are available, the private government of housing through homeowners' associations (HOAs) and deed covenants and restrictions constitute important (and legal) exclusionary practices, but have been collected systematically only in a few metropolitan areas. There has been work on the topic, much of it based on metropolitan case data (Danielson, 1976; Berry, 2001), or aggregated metro-level data (Pendall, 2000; Berry, 2001; Pendall, Puentes, and Martin, 2006). Glaeser and Ward (2009), for example, assembled a database of municipal land-use

regulations from the Greater Boston area. The interaction of transportation programs and land-use policies is worthy of substantial additional research.

30 Of course, transit buses occasionally use expressways, but this is rare.

31 For a discussion of the postwar trends in transit use, see Jones (2008), who nicely highlights how urban transit ridership was already in decline before World War II, and only momentarily spiked due to wartime driving restrictions and fuel rationing. See also Pucher (2004, 207–8). Even as transit has been in decline as a middle-class service, it has remained an important social service for low-SES Americans.

32 Sanchez et al. (2007) discuss the socioeconomic biases associated with specific transportation modes (43–44).

33 These data are available only in the restricted-use data set. While the particular zip code database used to assign YPSPS addresses is not reported, a check against historical zip code directories from 1967 and 1982 indicates that the zip codes are from later in the study period. For this reason, I use 2004 zip code goegraphic information system (GIS) boundary files. Note that the 1965 zip code used matches the address of the respondent's high school, not the respondent's home address.

34 This included respondents from counties surrounding the one hundred most populous US cities in 1950.

35 A 10-mile buffer around Interstates defines a reasonably large neighborhood while only including areas with easy highway access.

36 Low-income respondents had less than $7,000 income, middle-income residents $7,000–$15,000 income, and higher-income residents had income greater than $15,000 per year in 1973 (in their late twenties).

37 To reduce bias resulting from panel attrition, missing values were imputed using the Amelia II R package (Honaker, King, and Blackwell, 2011).

3 | Highways Polarize Metropolitan Political Geography

As Chapter 2 demonstrated, partisans have differed in their community preferences, and transportation infrastructure enables them to act accordingly. In this chapter, I demonstrate how the Interstate Highway System, specifically, has changed the political makeup of metropolitan areas since the 1950s. By facilitating suburban growth and migration, highways have enabled suburban Republican growth, especially in fast-growing counties concentrated in the South and the Sun Belt. Because of the Interstate Highway System, the central and peripheral counties of metropolitan areas have become more polarized from each other than they would have been otherwise.

The Interstate Highway System offers an ideal case study for examining transportation infrastructure's effects on political geography. First, it was large in scope (41,000 miles in length, as originally planned), and most of this mileage was built in the first decade or so after passage of the Federal Aid Highway Act of 1956. Second, the Interstate Highway System was a preplanned and plausibly exogenous intervention: while state governments had discretion over localized details of highway routing, unlike previous legislation, the Federal Aid Highway Act of 1956 funded a single, nationwide highway network. State highway engineers, often operating strategically to satisfy the preferences of state and federal officials, nominally relied upon documented criteria when determining where to locate roads (Seely, 1987).[1] While meddling by elected officials may sometimes explain the rules under which highways were placed in some counties and places and not others (the "assignment mechanism") (Rubin, 1991), this process can be reconstructed for Interstates far more easily than for many other types of policy interventions.

The widely publicized factors used in planning the Interstate Highway System facilitated an estimation strategy employing nonparametric matching and regression to identify Interstate highways' effects. Much of my attention in this chapter focuses on the factors leading to

Interstate placement in one place versus another. Unlike other highway programs, a single Interstate plan was adopted in broad outline before construction, enabling present-day researchers to identify and then account for the factors driving nonrandom highway placement. Key planning criteria to be used in the locations of a national expressway network appear in the 1944 *Interregional Highways* report, which laid out an early version of what would become the Interstate Highway System (United States, Public Roads Administration, 1944). Many of the factors most important in dictating intercity expressways' general location are accounted for in this report, and informed highway planning well into the 1960s. State highway engineers working in cooperation with the federal Bureau of Public Roads (later, the Federal Highway Administration) enjoyed substantial autonomy in the planning and execution of roads on the Interstate network.[2]

Here, I present results of two quantitative case studies, which together provide evidence of highway-induced suburban change and associated urban–suburban polarization. Two closely related statistical methods, nonparametric matching (Ho et al., 2007; Iacus, King, and Porro, 2011) and least squares regression, enabled me to determine the extent to which Interstate highways made suburban counties in which they were built more Republican than they would have been otherwise. I show that highways' effects varied across regions, with the South appearing to be the epicenter of these changes (Nall, 2015). After demonstrating highways' influence on the political composition of suburban counties, I report their effects on metropolitan areas as a whole, showing that denser highway networks result in more partisan polarization between top metropolitan areas' urban and suburban counties. One of the key findings reported in this chapter is that such highway-induced political changes in the suburbs were typically largest in already fast-growing metropolitan areas. These fast-growing areas, primarily but not exclusively located in the South, have seen a larger increase in their polarization over time.

Interstates and Partisan Change in Suburban Counties

I begin by examining highways' effect on suburban counties' partisan composition since passage of the Federal Aid Highway Act of 1956, exploiting geographic information system (GIS) data on the location of highways to see the effect placement of an Interstate highway in a county affected the county's partisan makeup. To accomplish this, I combined GIS data on the expansion of the Interstate system (Baum-Snow, 2007*a*) with data from the National Historical GIS and other historical political and Census databases (Fitch and Ruggles, 2003).[3] Data on the location of highways comes from a Federal Highway Administration (FHWA) database of Interstate construction through 1996. Each county in the data set has Census data through 1950 and county-level Democratic share of the presidential vote from 1948 to 2008, thus allowing estimation of the effects of expansion of the highway system by matching comparable suburban counties and examining highways' effect on suburban development over time.

Data and Methods

The analysis in this section is focused on suburban counties, defined as those whose centers (geographic "centroids") are within a set distance from the major central city (or cities) in a metropolitan area. I define metropolitan areas, and the suburban ring that surrounds them, in terms of *catchment areas* around which daily commuters may choose to live, even if such areas were not populated at the time Interstate highways were being built. Suburban counties are defined as those with geographic centroids 20–100 kilometers from the center of the one hundred most populous cities in 1950.[4] While any definition of urban and suburban based on radius from a city center is arbitrary, a radius of 100 kilometers captures an area that could be approximately covered by a one-hour commute from the central city at current typical Interstate highway speeds. This catchment area thus represents the region around each city at risk of highway-induced suburban development.[5]

Relying on county data permits longitudinal comparisons that are untenable using more contemporary, fine-grained data. Although precinct-level presidential election results (e.g., King and Palmquist, 1998; Ansolabehere and Rodden, 2012) or commercial voter lists (Ansolabehere and Hersh, 2012) provide much more detail about the geographic distribution of partisans, they are often lacking in other respects. Precinct-level data are rarely available from years prior to the widespread adoption of GIS technology around the year 2000. Counties, by contrast, have many advantages for the purposes here.

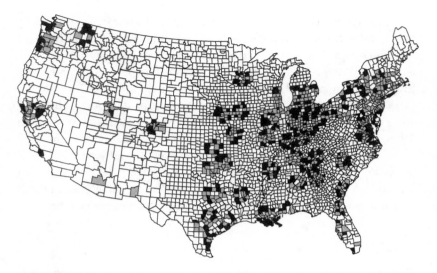

Figure 3.1. Map of the suburban county sample used in analysis of highways' role in suburban partisan change. Counties containing an Interstate highway through 1996 are lightly shaded and others included in the sample are shaded black.

They are geographically stable, facilitating longitudinal comparisons. They are also responsible for delivering important public services, including local roads, transit, education, and social welfare programs, making them units of interest in their own right. The full suburban county sample of $n = 988$ used in matching and regression analyses appears in Figure 3.1.[6]

In addition to facilitating causal analysis, Interstate highways (and other infrastructure) have a unique feature relevant to any longitudinal analysis: they persist long after initial construction, meaning that they will influence residential choice for decades after their original placement, and as local political conditions change. For example, a highway built in 1960 would influence a county's social, economic, and political development twenty years longer than one built in 1980.[7]

To account for the importance of construction timing, highways were coded as being built in one of three "treatment" periods: the initial period of Interstate construction (1956 through 1963);

the middle period of highway construction (1964 through 1971), after which most Interstate highways were completed; and a late period of highway construction (1972 through 1979). For each of these periods, I report how Interstate highways changed counties' Democratic share of the presidential vote over time. Most Interstates were built during the politically unconstrained highway construction boom that lasted from 1950 to the late 1960s – a period that Altshuler and Luberoff (2003) label as part of the "great mega-project era." In later years, localized opposition to highway building and growing environmental and community activism impeded highway construction (though most highways were already finished by the third period). Among the counties that would eventually have any Interstate highways, 51 percent had at least one Interstate segment by 1965 and nearly all (96 percent) had one by 1980.

For each of these periods, a county is defined as "treated" if at least one Interstate highway opened during the chosen treatment period, as reported in the PR-511 data.[8] For each of the three initial construction periods, highways' effect on the Democratic share of the presidential vote through 2008 is reported.

Of course, highways are not built in counties at random; perhaps suburban counties that built highways were those that were already more likely to become less Democratic. To account for the factors that led to nonrandom assignment of highways to counties, I first matched comparable treated and untreated counties in each time period, using coarsened exact matching (CEM) to create a balanced sample.[9] I then fitted a least squares regression in each year to each matched sample using the same treatment variables and covariates used in matching (Ho et al., 2007; Iacus, King, and Porro, 2011). The result of this subclassification and trimming of the sample yields a local estimate for treated observations that could be well matched.

County-level Census and political variables used in matching and in the least squares regression included criteria from *Interregional Highways*, widely regarded as the foundational planning document for the Interstate Highway System. The model also accounts for potential confounders related to intervention in the highway-building process. Among the variables included in the model were *population density*, *crop value per capita, percentage urban in 1950* and the *number of manufacturing establishments in 1939*, all reported by the Census and mentioned in some fashion in the 1944 report.[10] A dummy variable for *strategic route* was also included to indicate whether a county was on or near a "strategic military route" in 1941 (United States, Public Roads Administration, 1944, 33).[11]

Other covariates represent potential confounders related to preexisting migration patterns. *Median family income in 1950* was included as it is predictive of automobile ownership, suburban residential development, and partisanship. The *percentage of 1950 families that lived outside the county in 1949* was included to capture baseline suburban migration trends. *Percentage nonwhite in 1950* is a strong correlate of both partisanship and future partisan change. To account for pretreatment trends in the presidential vote and to capture secular trends in partisan change, the county-level *Republican presidential vote shares in 1948 and 1952* were also included in each regression. To account for confounding political trends between the time Interstate highways were assigned through legislation and when they were actually built in each of the three treatment cohorts, the presidential vote in the first year of each treatment cohort is included as a control variable.[12] Matching on these variables greatly reduces imbalance between treated and untreated suburban counties on most covariates in most posttreatment years.[13]

To account for regional heterogeneity, I first perform this matching and regression analysis for all suburban counties and then separately for Southern and non-Southern suburban counties. In the nationwide analysis, a dummy variable for the *South* was included to account for southern legislative influence over highway policy and the Southern realignment, which coincided with highway-induced suburbanization. The same variable was used to divide the sample into Southern and non-Southern subgroups, and the matching procedure was applied separately to both regional samples.[14]

Regression models were fitted to each matched sample generated for each treatment cohort, posttreatment election year, and region estimated Interstates' effect on the Democratic percentage of the two-party vote using least squares regression, starting in the election years immediately after each treatment period (1964, 1972, and 1980, respectively) through 2008:

$$\mathbf{Y_t} = \beta_{0t} + \beta_z \mathbf{z} + \beta_{1t} \mathbf{x}_1 + \ldots + \beta_{kt} \mathbf{x}_k + \epsilon \qquad (3.1)$$

where Y_t is the county Democratic presidential vote share in year t, and $\mathbf{z}$ is a dummy variable representing whether an Interstate was built in the county under the specified treatment cohort.[15] The coefficient β_z captures the effect of interest in year t, and $x_1 \ldots x_k$ represent additional pre-treatment variables previously described.[16] To construct accurate confidence intervals, and to account for election-specific deviations from the Democratic normal vote, I bootstrapped and lowess-smoothed election-specific effects to produce 95 percent and 80 percent confidence intervals.[17]

Results

The results of this estimation strategy indicate that Interstate highways made suburban counties in which they were built less Democratic across most of the study period, though these effects vary across both time and region. The largest effects arose from Interstates constructed in the first period and in. the South (Figure 3.2), though smaller, measurable effects appeared even outside the South. On average, a suburban county that had an Interstate built between 1956 and 1963 (the initial boom period in highway construction) became 2–3 points less Democratic during a period extending for several decades. Interstates' effect on – suburban political change differed by region, with a much larger and persistent 5- to 7-point effect in Southern suburban counties. Effects in non-Southern counties were smaller and less persistent, though the Interstate highways built earliest made non-Southern counties 1–2 points less Democratic than they would have been otherwise across the years 1980 and 1996.

Why Are Effects So Large in the South?

Interstates' effects on the suburban Democratic vote were larger in the South, and it is worth asking whether the region's longstanding deviation from political trends observed in the rest of the country was responsible or if the postwar modernizing South was merely at a different stage in its economic and political development (Shafer and Johnston, 2006). I consider three possible explanations for the large effects in the South. The first is that the "Solid South" became much less solidly Democratic across the period under study, with white voters shifting to the Republican Party over decades and white Republicans immigrating from outside the South. The resulting

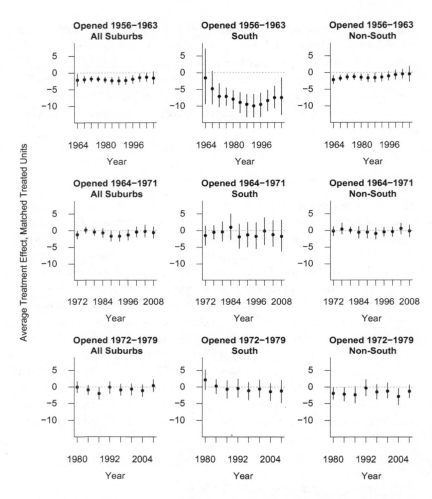

Figure 3.2. Smoothed ordinary least squares (OLS) estimates of effect of Interstate on the Democratic vote in suburban counties, using matched samples. Interstate highways reduced the suburban proportion of the Democratic presidential vote, with the strongest effects appearing early on and in the South. Ninety-five percent confidence intervals accompany each estimate. Top row: Interstates opened 1956–1963. Middle row: Interstates opened 1964–1971. Bottom row: Interstates opened 1972–1979.

realignment of white voters meant that suburbs with additional white in-migration (brought about in part by highways) would have undergone a larger secular partisan shift as a result. However, this phenomenon was not limited to the Solid South, as different groups of white voters were moving to suburbs and becoming more Republican across all regions of the country, including in non-Southern areas such as Orange County, California (McGirr, 2001). Another possible explanation is that non-Southern suburban counties included in the sample were already more developed, and thus observed sectional heterogeneity simply reflects other baseline differences in the regional samples. In 1950, for example, Southern suburban counties had an average population density of fifty-three persons per square mile, versus ninety-one persons per square mile in non-Southern suburbs. This appears to be a large difference that could explain the different results obtained in Southern and non-Southern counties, but except for a few counties in the Northeast and Rust Belt, most suburban-sample counties were predominantly rural in 1950. In fact, preexisting development of counties at baseline (as measured by population density) had little bearing on highways' political effects.

The major sectional differences appear to have had as much to do with pretreatment growth trends in counties as with region-specific trends. To address this point, I stratified the analysis to ascertain whether effect sizes differ as counties grow in population. One of the main reasons that Southern suburban counties (as well as Sun Belt counties of the West) became more Republican in the postwar period was that high growth rates attracted northern Republicans, and economic growth stimulated emergence of modern suburban communities. Such counties also experienced white flight from Southern cities (Black and Black, 2002; Shafer and Johnston, 2006; Hillygus, McKee, and Young, 2017). Such high-growth counties were not limited to Southern states, but they were disproportionately located in the southern half of the country.

Highways were, in part, responsible for these growth disparities, which persisted after highways were built. Looking at average population growth rates in the sample between 1950 and 2000, suburban counties with Interstates grew 185 percent, while those without grew only 83 percent on average. Growth rates were higher in the South. Southern suburban counties on Interstates grew 224 percent, while those away from Interstates grew 93 percent. Non-Southern Interstate counties grew at a much slower 156 percent, while non-Southern non-Interstate counties grew by 76 percent.[18] In short, growth was more rapid in suburban counties with Interstates regardless of region, though Interstates' role in suburban growth was larger still in the South. The faster population growth coincided with social, economic, and partisan change.

One might wish to ascertain whether the pace of population growth reported here, partly brought about by highways, was part of the causal mechanism by which highways changed partisan geography. This mediated effect could be estimated here, but doing so introduces serious potential for bias, especially in an observational study (Rosenbaum, 1984; Imai et al., 2011). Even stratifying on baseline population change is risky, since many of the fastest-growing counties had Interstates but very few of the slowest-growing counties did, making a suitable controlled comparison even more difficult. To address both of these problems, I grouped sample counties according to *metropolitan-area* population growth between 1950 and 1960, using population data for all counties in the metropolitan catchment areas defined in the preceding analyses. I then estimated freeways' effects in 1964 and beyond within terciles of metropolitan population growth, 1950–1960, by region (Southern versus non-Southern states).

Limiting this check to the first cohort of Interstate construction to simplify interregional comparisons, in Figure 3.3 I present estimates of the effect of Interstate highways built between 1956 and 1963 versus counties where Interstates were never built. I present the same linear regression models used to produce Figure 3.2, but using only least squares regression, and stratified by 1950s growth tercile and region. This method produces estimates comparable to those in the top row of Figure 3.2. This analysis shows that Interstate highways made counties in fast-growing metropolitan areas more Republican regardless of region, while this effect was non existent, and perhaps even negative, in slow-growing areas.[19] The large effects in fast-growing metropolitan areas of the South *and* non-South suggest that the pace of metropolitan growth drove partisan change in the suburbs. Highways' opposite effect in slow-growing metropolitan areas outside the South likely resulted from two factors: the sectional realignment in which Northeastern Republicans shifted to the Democratic Party and the fact that non-Southern inner suburbs (already developed suburban

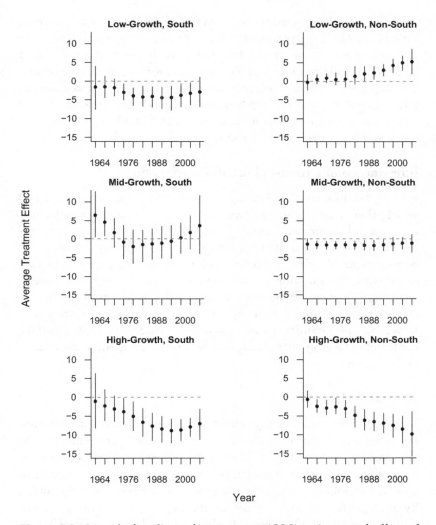

Figure 3.3. Smoothed ordinary least squares (OLS) estimates of effect of Interstate on the Democratic vote in suburban counties, by region and pre-treatment metropolitan-area growth rates. The "South" regional effect, while important, reduces dramatically when pre-Interstate metro-area growth rates (1950–1960) are taken into account. For simplicity, this analysis focuses on Interstates built between 1956 and 1963 (the treatment cohort with the largest overall effects). Ninety-five percent confidence intervals accompany each estimate.

counties with aging housing stock) were racially diversifying (see, e.g., Orfield, 1994).[20] Interregional differences do not appear to have been as large after accounting for baseline growth: the highway-induced Republican shift was larger in high-growth areas, regardless of region. The Sun Belt (especially fast-growing Southern states such as Georgia, Florida, and Texas) was much more likely to have such areas, and those with Interstates grew more rapidly and shifted more strongly in the Republican direction as a result.

Interstates and Urban–Suburban Polarization

Having established that Interstates made the suburban counties in which they were built less Democratic over time (with suburban counties in high-growth, mostly Southern and Sunbelt areas accounting for most of these effects), I now turn to highways' role in the development of urban–suburban polarization. The previous section dealt with the question of differences *within* metropolitan areas' suburban rings resulting from Interstate highway construction. In this section, I examine highways' effect on political geography at a larger, metropolitan-level scale. I show that Interstate highways have contributed to growing polarization between metropolitan areas' core and periphery.

Data and Methods

I report Interstate highways' effect on urban–suburban polarization for urban and suburban counties from the same metropolitan areas analyzed in the last section. Metropolitan areas were constructed by forming "couplets" aggregating the urban and suburban counties in each metropolitan area. The urban portion of each was assembled by aggregating counties containing the one hundred most populous cities as of 1950, while the suburban remainder was assembled by aggregating all other counties with centroids up to 100 kilometers from each central city (or cities). This process yielded eighty-four urban–suburban couplets containing the one hundred major cities and their hinterlands. For each of these metropolitan areas, the urban–suburban difference in the Democratic vote share in each couplet was calculated. $\Delta_{i,t} = \bar{D}_{iut} - \bar{D}_{ist}$, where $\bar{D}_{iut}$ and $\bar{D}_{ist}$ represent, respectively, the urban and suburban Democratic vote share in the metro area i in year t.

To capture the overall density of highways in a metropolitan area, I constructed a new explanatory (treatment) variable to capture how well highways are connected with the local street grid (a necessary condition for facilitating of residential sorting): the number of *Interstate highway exits per square mile*.[21] This measure more accurately captures how highways contribute to economic and residential development on local streets and highways around freeway exits. The number of exits per highway mile has been surprisingly stable since the Interstate Highway System was built, since federal highway officials controlled construction of new exits to maintain express highways' "limited access" character.[22]

I used least squares regression to account for potential confounders of the exit "treatment," again referring to the *Interregional Highways* report to identify factors that might explain the density of exits within metropolitan areas. The most important of these was metropolitan-level population. Exits were placed on the Interstate system to provide access to street and road networks, which tended to be more substantial in cities and higher-population areas. Among variables in the reported models, *metropolitan area population density in 1950* captures this concentration of population. *Proportion of metropolitan area counties on a route of strategic military importance in 1941* measures the perceived military importance of each metro area, which may have factored into each route. The *mean number of manufacturing establishments in 1939* accounts for preexisting industrialization and is also a predictor of Interstate construction. The *lagged urban–suburban difference in the Democratic presidential vote share* in 1948, 1952, and 1956 captures pretrends in metropolitan-level political development. Because urban–suburban racial makeup is currently one of the strongest correlates of urban–suburban partisan polarization, it was incorporated into the models through *urban percentage nonwhite minus the suburban percentage nonwhite in 1950* and *metropolitan-wide percentage nonwhite in 1950*. A *South* dummy variable was added to models to account for preexisting regional differences in infrastructure and other pretreatment trends. Finally, economic prosperity at baseline was accounted for by including the *mean of median family income of counties across the metropolitan area*.[23]

I examine the effect of two versions of the highway exit density variable: the version previously described and a log-transformed version. These were estimated by least-squares regression:

$$\Delta_t = \beta_0 + \beta_{z_t} z_t + \beta_2 x_1 + \ldots + \beta_k x_k + \epsilon \qquad (3.2)$$

where β_{z_t} represents the effect of a one-Interstate-exit-per-square-mile (or the natural logarithm of the Interstate exit per square mile) difference in exit density at year $t - 4$, with $x_1, \ldots, x_k$ included as controls. The analysis otherwise follows the same bootstrapping and smoothing procedure used in the suburban-county analysis.[24]

Results

Figure 3.4 plots the predicted first differences in the urban–suburban Democratic voting gap associated with a typical increase in Interstate exit density (a shift from the 25th to 75th percentile, using 1996 sample quantiles throughout). The left panel of Figure 3.4 displays this effect for the exit-density variable, the right panel its log-transformed version. As these results show, higher Interstate density in a metropolitan area has been associated with greater urban–suburban polarization in the presidential vote. Point estimates are uniformly positive under both versions of the exit-density variable, and, in both

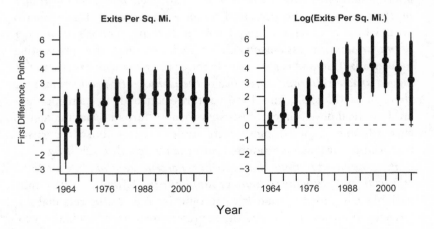

Figure 3.4. Interstate highways' effect on the urban-suburban Democratic presidential vote gap, comparing across the interquartile range of exits per square mile in 1996. Left: exit density. Right: log-transformed exit density. Bootstrapped 80 percent and 95 percent confidence intervals accompany the estimates.

models, the 95-percent confidence interval indicates that highways had a measurable effect by around the 1970s. The predicted first difference across the interquartile range is somewhere between 2 and 4 percentage points across most of the study period.[25]

Conclusion

For the past half-century, Democrats and Republicans have increasingly separated on an urban-to-suburban continuum. Interstate highways have been a driver of these changes, shaping numerous aspects of metropolitan life, including the political makeup of communities. Built at a point of rapid social and economic change during the postwar era, Interstates facilitated ongoing suburbanization and white flight, contributing to a larger urban–suburban split where they were built. Interstates' effects were especially pronounced in regions that were already fast growing when Interstates arrived. This resulted in large effects in the realigning South, where counties with Interstates became 5 points less Democratic, on average. Overall, these highway-induced suburban changes contributed to steadily worsening urban–suburban polarization. In brief, the two parties in the electorate have not just become more politically sorted over this period (with Republicans adopting more consistently conservative positions and Democrats adopting more consistently liberal ones), they have also become more geographically sorted, with highways as a major enabler.

The effects found here are comparable to other effects on voting outcomes in places. The difference in urban–suburban polarization associated with an increase in exit density across the interquartile range is about one-fourth as large as the average urban–suburban gap during the study period. The magnitude of effects is also similar to other observational estimates of public policies' effects on voting in presidential and congressional elections. For example, in Levitt and Snyder (1995), an increase in federal nontransfer spending of $100 per capita, or "approximately $50 million" per house district, was shown to boost House member vote share by about 2 percentage points. Another study found that presidential disaster declaration adopted in a state increases the incumbent president's vote share by 1 point (Reeves, 2011, 1150). Unlike these other widely analyzed interventions, which are by design short-lived, highways' long-term effects are often larger and persist for decades after the initial highway construction. Interstates thus have the potential to "lock in" long-term political effects.

Highways helped to create a more polarized spatial order. While nearly all major metropolitan areas have highways, variation in the timing and placement of expressways also contributes to variation in the partisan geography of suburbs and of metropolitan areas as a whole. Under this new regime, partisanship has become even more clearly associated with urban and suburban place of residence. In this chapter, I have shown that this geographic distribution is due, in no small part, to the federal-aid highway program and its consequences for metropolitan political geography. In the next chapters, I show why this matters for reasons beyond presidential election maps or legislative or congressional polarization. Partisan geographic polarization plays a role in partisans' policy attitudes, shaping public policy in the process.

Notes

1 Rose and Seely (1990) write that highway engineers were adept at cultivating relationships with elected officials, including state legislators among whom engineers "enjoyed tremendous respect" (29–30). State highway department engineers often defended the scientific foundations of their field by citing tools of their trade – such as origin-destination studies – used to rationalize road construction plans (Mickle, 1952).

2 The politics of the Interstate program were, therefore, quite different from the ad hoc projects commonly studied in the distributive politics literature. One might raise the concern that technical criteria were merely used in post hoc justifications of politically motivated highway location decisions. Whether or not this was the case, accounting for these factors in the analysis would also account for whatever political manipulation or bias existed.

3 To assemble historical GIS data, Baum-Snow (2007*a*) geocoded project construction segments reported in the FHWA's PR-511 database.

4 At the baseline time period chosen for this study (the 1950 Census year), numerous metropolitan areas in the Sun Belt still had tiny populations, while major cities in the Rust Belt remained near the top of the city population rankings.

5 An issue that faces all geographic research is that geographies of interest can be defined by the researcher. In this case, the definition of a "metropolitan area" is sensitive to researcher choice (Rosenbaum, 1999). One might ask why I did not use existing metropolitan statistical

area (MSA) boundaries, which are defined by the Office of Management and Budget for cross-sectional planning purposes and widely used by social scientists. While present-day metropolitan boundaries are official and widely used, they are an outcome of the very highway-induced changes I am considering here. For example, in 1950, Detroit was the nation's fifth-largest city, with a population of 1.85 million, while Phoenix was the ninety-ninth-largest city with a population of only 106,000. Their positions are now substantially reversed. While the Detroit and Phoenix MSAs have about the same population, the developed area of Phoenix is much larger than it was in 1950. By the same token, using preferred metropolitan boundaries from 1950 would omit counties that subsequently developed because of the building of highways. An analysis of findings' sensitivity to radius choice and various population density thresholds appears in the online Supporting Information for Nall (2015).

6 The closest city center is defined using the point location in the StreetMap USA Cities layer. It is usually located in or near the central business district (ESRI, 2008). GIS data were projected using the North American Lambert Conformal Conic Projection.

7 While cities have on rare occasions removed highways, such freeway removals tend to occur over very short urban segments and not in suburban or rural areas.

8 Two dates are recorded in the PR-511 data: when construction began, and when a segment opened.

9 The CEM procedure trims the data in a manner that allows for estimation of a local average treatment effect on the included treated units. For each of the three treatment cohorts, for each region, and for each presidential election year following the treatment cohort, counties with an Interstate were matched to comparable counties in which an Interstate had yet to be built. I coarsened each covariate into at most three categories.

10 For modeling purposes, population density, which roughly captures urban versus rural interests, was log-transformed.

11 Urban legends have crept into public discussions of the history of the Interstate Highway System. "Military necessity," including alleged issues such as evacuation of cities in the event of a nuclear war, barely figured in the legislative history of the program. While the Pentagon supported the highway program, military concerns were never paramount. Richard Weingroff, the de facto Federal Highway Administration historian, has written about a number of other persistent myths around the program (United States. Department of Transportation. Federal Highway Administration, 2017).

12 Findings that omit this variable appear in the online Supporting Information for Nall (2015).

13 The standardized differences in means for each treatment cohort, region, and election year appear in the online Supporting Information for Nall (2015).

14 In effect, this allows all covariates to vary by region.

15 This variable is non-time-varying for each treatment cohort.

16 Because the treatment variable is not time-varying, the results reported here rely only on variables that were pretreatment. Inclusion of variables from years after the pertinent highway construction cohort might have introduced posttreatment bias (Rosenbaum, 1984).

17 For each matched sample in each region-year, one thousand samples were drawn (with replacement) with a probability equal to the CEM matching weights (Iacus, King, and Porro, 2011). The linear regression model was estimated on the national and regional matched samples, yielding one thousand bootstrapped point estimates for the Interstate highway coefficient in each year. Each of the one thousand sets of annual estimates were regressed on election year using lowess, with span of one-third of the data points in the smoothing kernel and three "robustifying iterations" (Becker, Chambers, and Wilks, 1988). Quantiles of these smoothed simulations were used to construct 95 percent and 80 percent confidence intervals.

18 These numbers are the unweighted average of county growth rates in the referenced counties, not the population-weighted growth rate in the area covered by the counties. As a result, they reflect very high growth rates in previously low-population rural counties on suburban areas' peripheries.

19 This result may reflect neighborhood life-cycle in such counties, with older housing stock filtering down to lower-SES (and more Democratic) residents.

20 As I noted earlier, the large effects in the South may subside over time. As more diverse, and Democratic groups move to the South, a new wave of more Democratic migration is likely – including migration of African Americans and high-education whites to some Southern metropolitan areas – to offset the previously strong Republican shift (Frey, 2004).

21 To generate a count of historical exits, I merged the Baum-Snow PR-511 database, which is based on the Federal Highway Administration's records of the Interstate segments' opening date, with the 2008 ESRI shapefile of Interstate exits as of 2008. Using the count of exits from this combined shapefile, I calculated the density of exits per square mile of metropolitan land area.

22 A robustness check using Rand McNally atlases showed that few exits were added to Interstates after initial construction, even in Sun Belt cities where rapid growth might have justified them. See the Supporting Information for Nall (2015).

23 Within-couplet urban–suburban differences were calculated using population-weighted (for Census variables) or voter-weighted means (for election variables). The within-couplet means were calculated by taking the unweighted mean of the Census averages of the urban and suburban portions of each couplet.

24 One thousand samples were drawn, and β_{zt} was estimated on each, for each election year t. A small positive value, 10^{-4}, was added to each value before the logarithmic transformation to permit calculation, but this was only relevant in the earliest years of the program. The bootstrapped point estimates were smoothed by lowess, yielding a 1,000-by-13 matrix of smoothed point estimates. The point estimate and 80 percent and 95 percent confidence intervals were constructed from the simulation mean and quantiles.

25 Region-specific effects were estimated, but with extremely large confidence intervals due to small sample size.

4 | *Transportation Becomes a Partisan Issue*

Highways have contributed tor the geographic polarization of American partisans for the last fifty years. Up to this point, I have not delved into how geographic polarization matters for specific political and policy outcomes. Past work has suggested that migration into the suburbs and the associated suburban context drove suburban Americans to adopt more conservative policy attitudes tied to their material interests as suburbanites and their experience in the suburban social milieu (Gainsborough, 2001). Without seeking to resolve longstanding and unresolved debates over the nature of contextual and neighborhood effects, we can establish the degree to which partisanship (whatever its foundations) has become more strongly tied to policy attitudes, and how this has taken on distinctly geographic character. While urban–suburban polarization is likely to have consequences in numerous political domains, I focus on a public opinion topic germane to the idea of "policy feedback" implied in past scholarship: that highways have created locally focused issue publics that support specifically urban and suburban policies. Transportation policy itself seems most likely to lend itself to interest-based explanations for policy attitudes. We might expect support for different transportation policies to be associated with residence in a city, suburban, or rural area, and for place of residence to matter as much to opinions on these policy matters as their partisanship or ideology. However, this traditional view becomes more difficult to substantiate as partisan geographic polarization increases and Democrat and Republican political elites adopt more polarized rhetoric around transportation policy.

To address the changing roles of partisan attitudes and economic interest in transportation policy attitudes, I assembled historical survey data and collected original surveys measuring support for policies related to highways and mass transit, the two general categories of programs widely seen as competing transportation policy alternatives. These two issues have been marked by disagreement along

70

the urban–rural divide and by partisanship, with mostly suburban and rural Republican voters endorsing highway spending to the exclusion of mass transit and other, nonhighway urban transportation investments (Grunwald, 2015; MacGillis, 2016).

As urban–suburban partisan geographic polarization has risen, have we also observed the development of uniquely suburban and urban policy attitudes, or are observed policy attitudes primarily a result of Republicans adopting pro-highway and antitransit attitudes, and migrating into different areas with their polarized issue attitudes? While I do not have the historical data to answer the question of the origins of policy attitudes, I am able to examine the extent to which transportation has become a more partisan policy arena, versus one more clearly associated with personal economic considerations and place-based factors. I present analyses of results from ninety cross-sectional national surveys on transportation policy conducted since the 1950s. These surveys collectively show that attitudes toward transportation policy cannot be attributed merely to "place-based" interests, and that, to the extent such interests exist, they have become increasingly difficult to distinguish from considerations now clearly tied to partisanship. Nor, after accounting for partisanship, can disagreements over transportation policy be explained as commonly implied in descriptions of suburban policy attitudes: that white or more affluent Americans who are more likely to live in suburbs endorse highways and oppose transit. I show that Democrats and Republicans have increasingly disagreed over transportation policy, especially around transit and related nonhighway transportation alternatives. Additional, more detailed surveys that I conducted in 2013 and 2015 show that partisan disagreement is more likely to arise around transportation policies that are most clearly dedicated to providing means-tested or targeted services to the poor. Contrary to conventional wisdom, both Democrats and Republicans (whether urban or not) generally agree on the value of highway spending. However, by asking questions that deliberately highlight how highway spending conflicts with other transportation priorities, we can elicit more partisan disagreement, and yield surprisingly little additional disagreement on urban–rural lines (beyond what is already being captured by partisanship).

Beyond providing what may be the first comprehensive examination of changing public support for competing transportation alternatives reaching back to the early years of the Interstate highway era, this chapter also reveals how partisanship now matters even to seemingly minimally ideological and nonsalient topics such as transportation infrastructure. Indeed, partisan differences over specific transportation investments do not vary dramatically by place of residence. As a result, when Democrats and Republicans do differ over how to invest in transportation, the geographic distribution of partisans will be important to assembling support for competing transportation policies. In addition, to the extent that factors other than partisanship drive results, they are likely to reinforce urban–suburban polarization around transportation policy. For example, after accounting for partisanship's usually substantial substantial association with policy attitudes on contentious transportation issues, rural residence (or residence in a low-population-density zip code), nonwhite race, and, to a lesser degree, lower income predict support for specifically urban-targeted highway spending and programs targeted at the poor. But partisan identification looms large, especially when the policy questions can easily be linked to partisans' increasingly consistent ideologies (Levendusky, 2009).

What Can We Learn from Survey Questions on Transportation Policy Attitudes?

Attempting to measure Americans' attitudes on transportation policy is a task that must be approached with caution. Even on hotly debated topics, survey responses are likely to represent a set of attitudes rooted in vague predispositions, rather than deeply considered policy preferences (Bartels, 2003). While they may deal with its effects on a daily basis, Americans think infrequently about transportation policy, meaning that responses at any given moment may reflect only whatever considerations come first to mind (Zaller, 1992).[1] Nevertheless, researchers can still extract useful attitudinal information from survey questions on specific transportation policies. While Americans may have little knowledge of transportation finance and operations, nearly all Americans are beneficiaries of federal, state, and local transportation policies, and all Americans participating in the modern economy contribute to transportation programs directly or indirectly through fuel taxes. Thus, when asked to answer a survey question about transportation, Americans are likely to bring more lived experience to the question than they might for other policy topics.

Three factors are likely to guide Americans' responses on transportation policy questions: *pocketbook* considerations (personal economic interest), personal political *ideology*, and *group biases* applied to users of different transportation modes.

First, *pocketbook* considerations might drive their attitudes. For example, regardless of their political ideology, residents of high-density cities might use mass transportation or perceive indirect benefits (such as reduced traffic congestion) from others' use of mass transit. High-income suburbanites, who are more likely to drive their own cars, drive longer distances, and not use mass transit, may support highway investments while opposing transit. This logic would be consistent with policy-feedback reasoning (Pierson, 1993): that highways (or other transportation infrastructure) create highway-dependent constituencies that favor additional road spending. Under this model of behavior, we would expect support for highways to be higher in areas where highway users drive more miles, or where they are most reliant on highways, regardless of partisanship.

The problem facing interest-based, policy-feedback explanations is that observed geographic patterns of public support for a policy may arise because residents of an area share a dependence on a particular policy, or because homophily in residential selection leads ideological "birds of a feather" (McPherson, Smith-Lovin, and Cook, 2001) to move to the same areas, carrying with them specific ideologies that they apply to policy questions.[2] An additional challenge to rigorous testing of interest-based explanations for transportation policy attitudes is that most all Americans are reliant in some way on highways and automobiles, regardless of income, race, or urban–rural place. Only in extremely dense urban zip codes (such as those in Manhattan or downtown Chicago) do a majority of workers use transit for their daily commutes. For example, according to the American Community Survey's five-year estimates for 2007–2011, in only 113 zip codes do a majority of workers over the age of sixteen use transit to get to work, and 105 of these zip codes are located in the New York City metropolitan area. In fact, a transit mode share of greater than 10 percent indicates transit-heavy neighborhoods in most metropolitan areas. Adding to the difficulty of distinguishing ideologically driven attitudes from pocketbook interests, the average 2008 Republican two-party presidential vote share in the most transit-heavy zip codes was only 16 percent.

And yet, federal, state, and local governments continue to fund transportation services, including transit, that serve only a minority (and, in most metropolitan areas, a small minority) of the population, calling into question a naive interest-based explanation for transportation policy attitudes. A competing explanation is that support for different transportation programs may be driven by *ideology* tied to partisanship (Levendusky, 2009). Partisans have not only sorted themselves geographically over recent decades; they have also adopted more ideologically consistent social and economic policy attitudes. Democrats are more consistently liberal, Republicans more consistently conservative (Levendusky, 2009), and partisans may form more coherent policy positions as a result of the increasingly consistent policy reputations of the two parties (Sniderman and Stiglitz, 2012). While transportation policy rarely becomes a subject of active public partisan debate (perhaps because it is so rarely on the national agenda), liberal or conservative (increasingly, Democratic or Republican) views are increasingly extending into the transportation policy agenda.

While Americans may not think about transportation often, when they are asked about transportation policy they may draw upon their attitudes regarding more hotly contested issues (such as welfare policy and the environment) to transportation policy questions. For example, whether government should fund the purchase of additional public transit buses may rarely cross the survey respondents' minds. However, because buses are associated with the poor, respondents may see spending on buses as a form of welfare. Similarly, affluent liberal Democrats who never take transit might be expected to support investment in rail projects because they are more likely to use rail on rare occasions, or because they believe reduce automobile emissions or otherwise benefit the environment, regardless of their personal experience with transit or whether they believe they would personally benefit.

Third, even if Americans do not think all that regularly about transportation policy, *group biases* may combine with their parochial and pocketbook concerns to determine their survey responses. For example, the same people who oppose specific transportation investments (for example, extending bus lines to low-income housing projects) may oppose transit spending more generally because they see it as a form of welfare. Attitudes toward welfare, immigration, and similar policies, however, are tied to racial biases (Gilens, 1999). While perceptions of transit users are not measured in any of the national survey results reported in this chapter, we can account for the possibility of racial bias indirectly by considering how much respondent race predicts attitudes after partisanship, income, and rural place of residence are accounted for. Since transit policies often look like a form of welfare, we might expect to observe race to play a role in these attitudes.

Historical and Contemporary Survey Data on Transportation Policy Attitudes

To weigh these competing explanations of transportation policy attitudes, I present findings from historical and contemporary survey sources: a compendium of multiple decades of transportation policy attitude questions assembled by the Roper Center for Public Opinion Research archives and other survey organizations, as well as General Social Survey (GSS) spending items (1984–2014). These results demonstrate the increasing role of partisanship in transportation policy attitudes as Democrats and Republicans separated along urban–suburban lines. While transportation-related items in the Roper archive and on the GSS address highway and transit spending, they rarely touch on specific aspects of these policies. Nor have existing studies consistently prompted respondents to consider different transportation programs' competition over limited budget resources.[3] To improve on existing, archived studies of transportation policy attitudes, I also present results from two original surveys conducted in 2013 and 2015 that were explicitly designed to address how Americans respond to specific, sometimes competing transportation policy alternatives.

I used data from the Roper archives for survey items pertaining to support for spending on highways (or "roads and bridges") and mass transportation. These two policy topics reflect a primary axis of conflict in American transportation policy. They have also been the two most heavily surveyed transportation topics. The Roper Center has archived original microdata from surveys conducted by major commercial polling firms since the early days of modern commercial polling. To identify relevant survey questions, I performed multiple keyword searches related to transit and highways, identifying the set of all questions on national surveys that asked respondents about their support for highway or transit programs. For each of these surveys, I selected items that measured support for federal or state transit and highway spending.[4]

Separately, I assembled data from the General Social Survey (GSS) combined file (1972–2014), which includes a battery of questions that ask whether the federal government is spending "too much," "too little," or "the right amount" of money in generic issue areas ranging from foreign aid and national defense to law enforcement. Two items pertaining to transportation investments – "roads and bridges" and "mass transportation" – have appeared on the GSS since 1984 (Smith, Marsden, and Hout, 2015).

I augment these findings by presenting results based on two original recent cross-sectional surveys with more detailed questions intended to induce respondents to consider the various policy trade-offs and limitations associated with specific transportation policies. While these questions delve into policy details more than most other transportation policy survey questions, they were also written in layperson's terms, so as not to require extensive prior policy knowledge. The 2013 survey, which also included the conjoint items presented in Chapter 2, included five Likert-scale items designed to gauge support for hypothetical transportation policies that might, in some way, be subject to the urban–rural or ideological divide. The 2015 survey included a battery of twenty-four highly specific policy priorities that might have been included in the federal transportation bill then under consideration in Congress (though some of the listed policies were more credible policy alternatives than others). The 2015 study included a simplified "quick-fire" conjoint design that requires respondents to compare randomly drawn pairs of priorities from the list of twenty-four, requiring quick judgments about competing interests.

The Changing Link Between Partisanship and Transportation Policy Attitudes

I begin by presenting results based on Roper Center and General Social Survey data. Drawing on question responses from these two data sources, I examined the partisan differences in support for highways and transit, conditioning on the covariate data available in each collection (which varied in quality and coverage). In order to present a longitudinal meta-analysis of survey responses, I estimated separate least squares regression models in specific time periods by pooling all related survey outcome variables calculated across surveys, including self-reported party identification and relevant predictors that were available within each group of surveys. For survey items from the Roper archives, I focused on estimating partisan attitudinal differences, controlling for respondent race, an important factor in the politics of metropolitan spatial policy, and one that was approximately standardized across different survey experiments and the survey study period.[5] For the General Social Survey spending items, a larger set of consistent or comparable predictors was available in addition to partisanship. For these items, I separately estimated models predicting support for highways and transit, with race and place of residence entered as additive terms.

The results of the regressions models demonstrate the growing importance of partisanship to transportation attitudes after accounting for leading competing explanations. In each of the reported results, I display the first difference in support for highways and transit. To simplify reporting of the effects of other variables, I display the marginal effect of a substantively meaningful shift in each of the variables in the regression models. Since I use a linear probability model, this reported result is simply the coefficient on each listed variable, which captures the additive effect of the variable relative to the specified base condition.

The results, reported decade by decade in Figures 4.1 and 4.2, appear at first to provide minimal support for the idea of partisan disagreement over transportation. Across all decades in the Roper collection (Figure 4.1), Republicans and Democrats have supported highway programs in about equal measure. In early surveys on the subject in the 1950s (in which respondents were specifically asked about construction of a new national expressway system), both Democrats and Republicans expressed very strong support for highways. National transportation policy then received little attention in national surveys (judging by those retained by the Roper Center) until the early 1970s, when Roper surveys reported lower support for highway spending among both Democrats and Republicans. At the time, Republicans were in fact 6 points less likely than Democrats to support government investments in highways. Since then, Democrats and Republicans have been about equally likely to support investments in highways. Accounting for respondent race in the models did little to change this conclusion about the role of partisanship, though white respondents have been slightly more supportive of highway spending

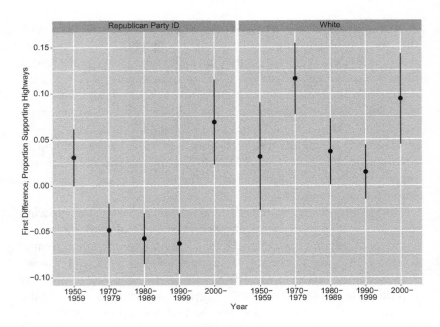

Figure 4.1. Results from linear probability models showing differences in support for highway programs on surveys collected in the Roper Center archives, by Republican partisanship (versus Democratic) and white (versus nonwhite) race.

after partisanship is accounted for. Since the 2010s, Republican partisanship has suddenly become a pronounced predictor of support for additional highway spending.[6] While recent surveys have shown that consistent majorities of Republicans and Democrats support highways, they suggest that even this bipartisan issue area has become partisan.

While the Roper meta-analysis indicates that highways still attract bipartisan support, surveys show that Republican party identification has increasingly become associated with opposition to mass transportation. In the mid-1970s, majorities of both Democrats and Republicans expressed support for spending on mass transportation. But, driven mostly by growing Republican opposition, the partisan gap grew in the 1980s. While few transit-related polls from the 1990s appeared in the collection, thereby minimizing what can be inferred about public opinion in that decade, the data indicate a long-term

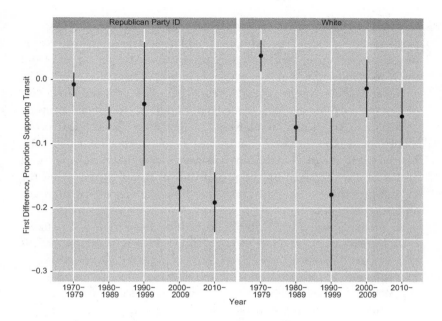

Figure 4.2. Results from linear probability models showing differences in support for transit programs on surveys in the Roper Center archives, by Republican partisanship (versus Democratic), and white (versus nonwhite) race.

decline in Republican support. By the 2000s, Republicans were 15–20 points less likely than Democrats to support mass transit. Moreover, it does not appear that this difference is merely a product of respondent race, which, when included in the model, does little to change the estimates of partisan differences. Racial differences existe, but these differences were much more variable, and, with the exception of one outlier survey from the 1990s, residual differences associated with white race (in addition to what can be captured by Republican partisanship) are in the single digits. Race and racial attitudes may, in fact, determine attitudes toward highways and transit, but they are expressing themselves most clearly through the partisanship of survey respondents. (Time-series cross-sectional data do not lend themselves to addressing the underlying mechanism.)

The Roper results indicate a growing partisan divide on transportation policy, but especially around mass transportation. However, other factors not measured on the Roper surveys might be explaining this partisan divergence. For example, population density, which is one measure of urbanism, was only sporadically available in surveys from the Roper collection, but was available in other series.

General Social Survey data (1984–2014) allow a more direct test of the partisan-ideological, place-based interest, and racial attitude hypotheses. Adopting a similar empirical strategy using linear probability models, I evaluate competing explanations by calculating marginal effects of Republican partisanship, white race, and rural versus urban residence on the proportion of respondents saying the federal government was spending "too little" money on either roads and bridges or transit.

Surprisingly, since 1984, Republicans have been slightly *less* likely than Democrats to say too little federal money is spent on "roads and bridges" (Figure 4.3). Over the same period, accounting for partisanship, population density, and income, the role of race in support for highways has surged, such that whites are now 10 points more likely to support road spending. However, just as the Roper surveys showed, support for highways has been generally bipartisan and highways have elicited support from city, suburban, and rural areas. After accounting for race and partisanship, rural residents have been only about 5 points more likely than urban residents to support spending on "roads and bridges." The GSS suggests that rural residence has been a stronger explanation than partisanship for attitudes towards highways. However, the level of support for road spending has been so high generally that a five-point urban–rural difference may be substantively inconsequential.

The GSS data do indicate that partisanship has shaped attitudes toward mass transit, possibly more recently than the Roper archive meta-analysis would suggest (Figure 4.4). Between 1984 and 1990, neither Republican identification nor white race explained support for federal mass transportation spending, though city (versus rural) residence did. The partisan difference grew gradually, then suddenly by the 2010s. In President Obama's second term, Republicans were 15 points less likely than Democrats to support transit, even after accounting for race and rural versus urban residence. In fact, beyond what is captured by partisan identification, nonwhite race was not a substantial additional factor explaining support for mass transit. In fact, after taking partisanship into account, white respondents

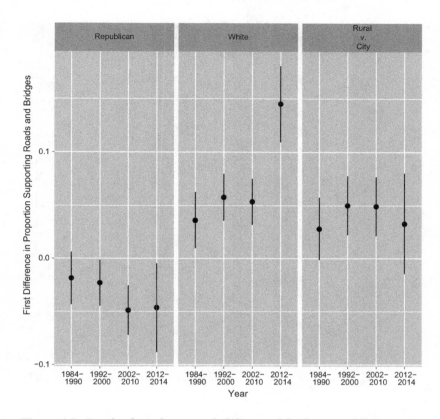

Figure 4.3. Results from linear probability models showing differences in support for "roads and bridges" spending on the General Social Survey, by Republican (versus Democratic) partisanship, white (versus nonwhite) race, and rural (versus city) residence.

expressed *higher* support for federal transit spending on the GSS series. Finally, across most of the GSS spending series, rural versus city residence was associated with about a 5-point drop in transit support, a meaningful amount but smaller than the recent partisan divide. If place-based interests did, in fact, become a more important factor shaping transportation attitudes, these interests, too, became bound up with partisanship. Partisan geographic sorting likely played a role in establishing this link.[7]

To be sure, care must be exercised in attempting to draw causal inferences about partisanship from the preceding results, which are

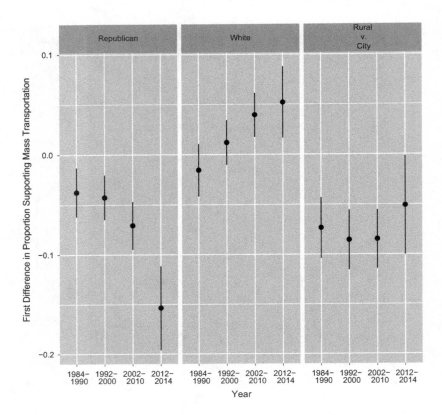

Figure 4.4. Results from linear probability models showing differences in support for mass transportation spending on the General Social Survey, by Republican (versus Democratic) partisanship, white (versus nonwhite) race, and rural (versus city) residence.

based on historical data with multiple limitations and regressions including sometimes highly correlated explanatory variables. Two factors may explain these results. The first is that the traditional city–suburban–rural distinction may not cause enough differences in transporation needs to yield meaningful differences in place-based interests. For example, population density, which is strongly predictive of transit and other nonautomobile travel, can vary substantially with subjective place categories (Meyer, Kain, and Wohl, 1971, ch. 6). "City" residents need not live in a high-density zip code or block group, for example. In itself, this points to a challenge facing mass transit proponents: all but a few Americans live in communities with population densities at which the automobile is the dominant and most convenient mode of transportation. Alternatively, if factors correlated with population density or urbanism are allowing interests to form around specific issues, an interpretation of the results is that place-based interests, while real, have not resulted in the formation of place-based issue publics (e.g., "highway-dependent suburbanites"). Whichever of these interpretations best applies, the results presented here show that transportation policy is becoming a much more partisan issue domain.

Evidence from Two Original Surveys

The Roper and General Social Survey data permitted a longitudinal analysis of changing transportation policy attitudes, but most of the included questions were posed in the most generic terms, preventing us from discerning the roots of partisans' changing attitudes. Highway and transit programs typically represent a bundle of subprograms that elicit different levels of support. I conducted two original online surveys to examine Americans' responses to facets of transportation policy that typically have not been addressed in national polls. The first, the Stanford Residential Preference Survey, was fielded online in 2013 on an online sample of 4,860 self-identifed Democrats and Republicans. In addition to posing questions about residential preferences used to produce the analyses in Chapter 2, the survey also included housing and transportation policy questions.[8] The second survey, conducted online in November 2015, reached two thousand respondents, and featured a simplified conjoint design under which respondents ranked multiple pairs of policies to be considered in a hypothetical pending federal transportation bill (Thurstone, 1927; Salganik and Levy, 2015). Unlike the GSS questions about spending on "roads and bridges" or "mass transit," these two surveys were written to measure attitudes on a wider range of policy problems and distributive and redistributive policy choices facing transportation policy makers while still being accessible to a layperson. The surveys were designed less to capture well-articulated policy preferences than to understand how Americans of different political stripes and with limited information about nonsalient issues approach transportation policy questions.

The 2013 survey asked respondents to state whether they strongly supported, somewhat supported, neither supported nor opposed, somewhat opposed, or strongly opposed each of the following:

- Building more lanes on major highways in central cities
- Building more lanes on major highways in suburbs
- Giving a tax break to people who drive their own cars to work
- Expanding urban bus service into the suburbs
- Using 20 percent of federal gas tax funds to pay for public transit[9]
- Building high-speed rail lines to connect major cities
- Providing special debit cards to the poor to help them pay for transportation

These responses were dichotomized so that "strongly support" or "somewhat support" were coded as 1, and a neutral attitude or any level of opposition was coded as 0.

The second survey, conducted in November 2015, addressed different ideas about highways and transit, as well as a number of ancillary transportation policy ideas. Each respondent viewed nine randomly generated pairs of policy priorities drawn from the list in Table 4.1. For each pair, respondents were asked, "Which should be a higher priority in the next federal transportation bill?" These provisions were not meant to be real policy options then being actively debated for the upcoming transportation bill, but to use the legislation to prompt respondents to think explicitly about trade-offs. Some policy items were included to elicit partisan differences over geographically targeted investment in urban, suburban, or rural areas, including transportation policies described as benefiting poor people or poor areas. Other choices clearly required deciding between competing transportation modes (highway, transit, and pedestrian).[10] An advantage of the paired design is that it put transportation policies into direct competition, albeit sometimes artificially.

The two surveys improved on previous opinion studies by incorporating fine-grained data concerning respondent place of residence, collecting zip-code data in place of the coarse codings of city, suburban, or rural residence that appear in other published studies.[11] While "urban" and "rural" have no set, uniformly accepted definition, throughout this analysis zip-code population density was used, because transit and other nonautomobile travel has tended to be correlated with higher population density. Density was grouped into

Table 4.1. *List of federal transportation policy ideas included in the online paired-comparison exercise.*

Repairing urban local streets
Repairing suburban local streets
Repairing rural local streets
Adding lanes to existing urban highways
Adding lanes to existing suburban highways
Adding lanes to existing rural highways
Buying new subways and trains for transit systems
Building new tunnels and stations for subway systems
Buying new buses for transit systems
General funding for light rail lines
Helping cities pay for downtown streetcars
Adding new bus routes connecting central cities to suburbs
Increasing the frequency of bus service between central cities and suburbs
Funding improved bus service at low-income housing projects
Providing debit cards to the poor to help them pay for their own
   transportation
Installing sidewalks to make neighborhoods more walkable
Light rail connecting cities and suburbs
Improving the frequency of bus service in the suburbs
Fixing structurally deficient bridges on major roads
Fixing structurally deficient bridges on minor roads
Improving "intermodal" systems to carry freight on trains, ships, and trucks
Repairing urban freeways
Repairing suburban freeways
Repairing rural freeways

three approximately equal categories: low (fewer than five hundred persons per square mile), middle (more than five hundred and fewer than seven thousand persons per square mile), and high (seven thousand persons per square mile or greater). Both surveys also included measures of race (white versus nonwhite racial identification), income (low-, middle-, and high-income),[12] and party. These variables were again included in linear probability models, which were used to generate estimates of the difference in predicted probabilities (i.e., first differences) associated with substantively meaningful changes in each explanatory variable.

Results

Responses to items on the 2013 and 2015 surveys again reveal a partisan pattern of support for different elements of transit and highway policy. They reveal why Democrats and Republicans disagree on transit funding but largely agree on highway funding and why these attitudes vary along urban–suburban lines. Figure 4.5 displays the 2013 survey results, summarizing the mean differences in support for each policy item by partisanship, as well as coefficient estimates from the full linear model. Consistent with previous published surveys, Democrats and Republicans have barely differed over new highway construction, even when policy details are more specific. Accounting for race, household income, and local population density, partisanship is unrelated to support for addition of lanes to city and suburban freeways (one of the key ways that expressways are expanded today), even though such highway expansions are often supported by Republican legislators and governors (Grunwald, 2015). Other policy items of interest to automobile users suggest that pro-automobile attitudes are not clearly tied to partisanship, income, or density. For example, both Democrats and Republicans supported a tax credit for automobile commuters, a decidedly pro-automobile policy. Nonwhite respondents were, in fact, more likely to favor such a tax break.[13]

Partisan differences were far more evident on questions related to transit, and repeatedly appear across survey items. On three transit-related items, Republicans were much less likely than Democrats to support protransit policies. After accounting for population density, income, and race, Republicans were 15 points less supportive of additional urban bus service to the suburbs, 20 points less supportive of diverting gas taxes to transit, and 20 points less likely to favor spending on high-speed rail.

The strong opposition to spending of federal gas taxes on transit is especially relevant, as it captures Republican voters' opposition to the status quo in federal transportation policy. Congressional transportation bills supported by members of both parties have consistently diverted about 20 percent of transportation trust fund outlays to mass transit since the mid-1970s (Altshuler and Luberoff, 2003, 187–8; Congressional Budget Office, 2015, exhibit 9).[14]

Where partisanship explains few policy differences we might expect population density or income to be driving attitudes on transportation policy issues, and this is borne out in the data to a limited degree.

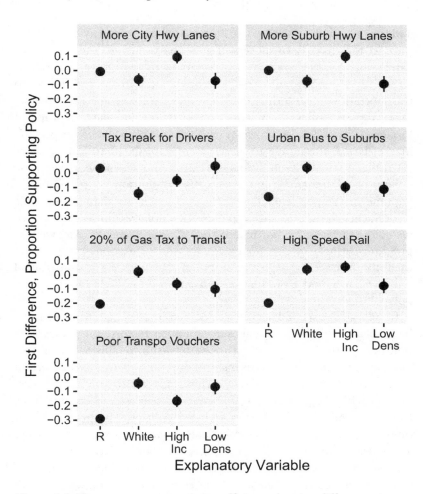

Figure 4.5. Least squares regression coefficients showing differences in support for different transportation policies by partisanship (Republican versus Democratic), income (high, defined as $85,000 and above versus low income, under $30,000), race (white versus nonwhite), and zip-code population density (fewer than five hundred persons per square mile versus greater than seven thousand persons per square mile). Source: Stanford Residential Preference Survey, June 2013 (Mummolo and Nall, 2017).

Democrats and Republicans largely agreed on building more highway lanes in cities and suburbs, but, after other factors were accounted for, higher-income respondents were more likely to favor them. Zip-code population density had no additional effect after party, race, and income were accounted for. Place-based interests may exist, but if they do, they have been subsumed under partisanship, and, to a lesser extent, income, race, and other nonspatial explanatory variables.

The 2013 study included additional questions pertaining to transportation ideas other than specific infrastructure investments. One of these policy ideas was transportation vouchers, a proposal broached by libertarian policy advocates, who favor a private, market-based alternative to government subsidy of transit agencies (O'Toole, 2010).[15] Republicans were 29 points *less* supportive of the policy than Democrats, and, even after accounting for partisanship, high-income respondents were 17 points less likely than low-income respondents to support such a policy. This polarization is substantial, on par with partisan and income-based disagreements over welfare programs; it also reveals the extent to which questions traditionally used to measure transportation policy attitudes have constructed only a narrow understanding of transportation policy's link to social policy.[16]

Results of the second survey (conducted in 2015) confirm the same basic relationship between partisanship, other factors, and transportation policy attitudes, showing that partisanship retains a central role but factors other than partisanship come into play around certain contested transportation policies. This study featured a set of questions in which Republicans and Democrats selected preferred policies from randomly generated pairs of listed policies. The proportion of time that an item was selected indicates that item's relative ranking. The paired comparison design required respondents to make choices that they might not make otherwise. While this induced a degree of artificial conflict, it also elicited disagreements that underlie divergent partisan attitudes on transportation policy.

I again used multiple regression models, this time estimating a model for each policy outcome to calculate the proportion of time each item was selected over a randomly drawn alternative. One of the key conclusions is that Democrats and Republicans agree on the relative importance of specific elements of transportation policy. Both Democrats and Republicans strongly prioritized basic maintenance and repair (such as repair of deficient bridges) over new construction. But on other items, and particularly those that entail geographic targeting of benefits to cities or rural areas or to the poor versus the rich, Democrats and Republicans disagreed more. They disagreed the most over transportation policies that were clearly described as benefiting the poor.

Figure 4.6 displays the multiple regression results for each item included in the paired tests.[17] To highlight the partisan preferences on different policy matters, policy items are ordered by the marginal effect of Republican (versus Democratic) partisanship after controlling for race, income, and population density. Policy measures that serve the poor, pedestrians, and transit users poll especially badly among Republicans. On the most polarizing policies, support is further diminished among members of groups (white, rural, and high-income) that are more likely to be Republican.

One benefit of including such a diverse list of policies in the paired-comparison test is the ability to discern partisan differences over the specific geographic distribution of transportation investments. For example, while both Democrats and Republicans both strongly favored infrastructure repair (versus new construction), Republicans were more likely than Democrats and their associated groups to support repair and expansion of *rural* roads and highways. Even after accounting for included demographic and contextual variables including population density, several policies are susceptible to substantial partisan disagreement.[18] Republicans were 18 points less likely than Democrats to support transportation vouchers, 13 points less likely to support bus service to low-income housing, and 8 points less likely to prioritize subway stations and tunnels. They were much more likely than Democrats to support programs designed to benefit rural and suburban areas: 12 points more likely to support repair of urban freeways, 10 points more likely to support repair of rural streets, and 8 points more likely support additional lanes on suburban highways. Importantly, these differences appeared even after controlling for income, race, and zip-code population density.

For policies on which Democrats and Republicans already substantially disagreed, the other explanatory variables had an additional effect on policy attitudes. For example, after accounting for party, income, and residential density, white respondents were less supportive of city-to-suburb buses (−9 points) and transportation vouchers for the poor (−7 points), but more supportive of repairing rural freeways (+7 points), repairing bridges on major roads (+7 points), suburban street repair (+7 points), and repairing bridges on minor roads (+6 points). Accounting for party, income, and race, residents of low-density zip codes were much less likely than residents of high-density zip codes to

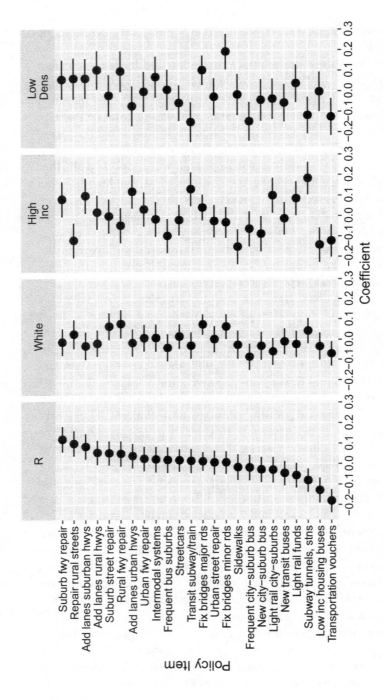

Figure 4.6. Least squares regression coefficients showing differences in support for various transportation policy items against randomly matched alternatives drawn from the same list. Marginal effect of Republican partisanship (versus Democratic), income greater than $80,000 (versus income less than $30,000), white (versus nonwhite), and low population density. Source: Author's survey, November 2015.

support more city-to-suburb buses (–15 points), subways and trains (–15 points), and transportation vouchers (–13 points). They were more supportive of repairing bridges on minor roads (+19 points), adding lanes to rural highways (+10 points), and repairing bridges on major roads (+10 points). These results indicate at least a degree of place-based policy interests, when policies are framed in a more specific way and geographically targeted options are put into direct competition.

One surprising result is that higher-income respondents were more likely to support certain urban and metropolitan investments. They were especially likely to support new transportation infrastructure (whether highways or transit) that tend to benefit middle- and upper-class users. They appear more likely than low-income respondents to support policies associated with *capital* investments in urban-area transportation but not programs designed for the poor. Relative to low-income respondents, high-income respondents were less likely to support prioritizing sidewalks (–15 points), buses to low-income housing projects (–14 points), transportation vouchers for the poor (–12 points), repair of rural streets (–12 points), more frequent suburban bus service (–10 points), and new city–suburb bus routes (–9 points). At the same time, all else equal, high-income respondents were more likely to support adding subway tunnels and stations (+18 points), transit subways and trains (+13 points), lanes to urban highways (+12 points), light rail between cities and suburbs (+11 points), and lanes to suburban highways (+10 points). This mix of policy attitudes is somewhat difficult to characterize, but it suggests that high-income people are, after accounting for their party identification and residential population density, more likely to embrace transportation *infrastructure* development, even if they are no more disposed (and sometimes opposed) to support transportation aid programs designed for pedestrians or the poor. This result is also consistent with prior work on the formation of the original federal coalition in support of transit in the 1960s and 1970s, which was heavily backed by a bipartisan coalition of middle- and upper-income transit users in the Northeast (Altshuler and Luberoff, 2003, 187–8).

Overall, the results of the conjoint paired-comparison test yield somewhat different conclusions about the role of partisanship than the other studies, showing that it is a primary factor, but one of many that arise in an observational analysis of transportation policy preferences. Policy debates sometimes require direct head-to-head choices, as often they involve compromises that can produce even more resources for supporters of competing policies. These artificial comparisons may, as a result, foster a differentiation in attitudes because choices are forced. At the same time, they can magnify underlying preferences that are motivating responses on more general questions about highways and transit. With a few exceptions, these differences are driven by attitudes tied to traditional liberal and conservative ideology, which is increasingly tied to, and captured by, partisanship.

Conclusion

The national surveys analyzed in this chapter demonstrate the critical role of polarized partisan geography in predicting where and how Americans are likely to embrace specific transportation policies. The idea that transportation is a bipartisan "policy-free zone," or defined by the principle of "no Democratic roads or Republican roads," has held true among many Washington policy makers or in the halls of Congress (Panagopoulos and Schank, 2007), but it is increasingly untrue of voter attitudes. While it is difficult to establish the causal pathway of attitudinal changes, as Democrats and Republicans have become more polarized along urban–suburban lines, they have also become divided over competing transportation policy alternatives. While these attitudes cannot be definitively connected to the changing geographic distribution of voters, this shift has occurred as the Republican electorate has become less urban. Republicans and Democrats alike support highways, but Republican voters have increasingly turned away from mass transit and other nonhighway transportation alternatives. This result may be due to their increasingly consistent attitudes toward redistribution, or because specific attitudes toward urban and rural investment are now being adopted by partisans regardless of their place of residence. The partisan divide around transportation policy appears to be larger the more a specific feature of policy is focused on delivering transportation policy specifically to the poor or to cities.

This growing partisan divide over transportation policy cannot easily be explained away just by race or by Republicans' tendency to live in low-density communities. When partisans are pressed to make forced choices over transportation policies, partisanship is the dominant factor explaining differences over major transportation controversies. While Democrats and Republicans agree on a range of transportation investment alternatives, they disagree most significantly on transportation policies that explicitly involve redistribution and targeting of transportation funds to the poor. Moreover, even when partisanship does not predict disagreement, other traits correlated with partisanship, including race, income, and place of residence, differentiate policy supporters. These results are consistent with past research suggesting that nontargeted social policies attract less controversy and more robust support than targeted means-tested or targeted policies (Skocpol, 1991). If Americans have viewed highways as a universalistic policy and mass transit as a poverty program, it may go far in explaining the political robustness of the former and the limited financial support of the latter.

While this chapter has presented many descriptive results linking partisanship and transportation policy attitudes, it has not attempted to ascertain partisanship's causal effect on attitudes. However, causal identification is not necessary to demonstrate how partisans' geographic distribution is likely to create different bases of policy support for public policies. These analyses have helped to explain how people are likely to become sorted – both by party and by geography – when establishing attitudes toward locally significant policies. One reading of these results is that the "nationalization" of policy attitudes (Hopkins, 2014) via partisan identification seems to be extending even into policy domains widely regarded as local and parochial.

Transportation policy appears, at first glance, to be nonsalient and the subject of bipartisan agreement. Beneath the surface, however, partisan dividing lines lurk, waiting to be activated by local controversy or by aspects of transportation policy that elicit an ideological response. On topics ranging from public transit to explicitly means-tested transportation programs, transportation policy attitudes are set along on partisan lines. When partisans are also *geographically* polarized on urban–suburban lines, we might expect these preferences to manifest themselves in voting on transportation referenda, in the behavior of elected officials, and in the operation of representative political institutions in metropolitan areas. The following chapters provide additional observational evidence indicating that partisan geographic polarization is important to the development of urban–suburban policy disputes and the distribution of transportation benefits and mobility in American cities.

Appendix

Survey Questions Used in Historical Transit Analysis

Year	Institution	Roper ID

1   1974   Roper Organization   USRPRR1974-01
Turning now to the business of the country – we are faced with many problems
in this country, none of which can be solved easily or inexpensively. I'm going to
name some of these problems, and for each one I'd like you to tell me whether you
think we're spending too much money on it, too little money, or about the right
amount ... Improving public transportation. Too much, too little, about right, or
don't know? (1 = too little, 0 = too much or about right, else coded NA)

2   1974   Roper Organization   USRPRR1974-02
Let's turn now to the question of public transportation. I'm going to name some
different methods of transportation, and for each one would you tell me whether
you think it is something that should get more financial support than it's getting,
less support, or has about the right amount of support now. ... City bus and
subway systems. (1 = more support, 0 = less support or about right, NA = don't
know)

3   1974   Roper Organization   USRPRR1974-08
There are a number of things that have changed rather drastically over the past
20 years. Here is a list of some of them. Would you read down that list and for
each one tell me whether you'd like to see continued advances and developments
on it in the future, or whether you think we've gone as far as we should on it
now, or whether we've already gone too far on it now. ... Methods of local public
transportation (buses, subways, etc.) (1 = would like continued advances, 0 = gone
as far as we should or too far, NA = don't know)

4   1975   Roper Organization   USRPRR1975-01
Turning now to the business of the country – we are faced with many problems
in this country, none of which can be solved easily or inexpensively. I'm going to
name some of these problems, and for each one I'd like you to tell me whether you
think we're spending too much money on it, too little money, or about the right
amount ... Improving public transportation. Too much, too little, about right, or
don't know? (1 = too little, 0 = too much or about right, else coded NA)

5   1976   Potomac Associates   USPOTM1976-GO7649
Now again remembering that government spending has to be paid for out of our
taxes, let me mention some other types of programs and ask whether you think
the amount of tax money being spent for each purpose should be increased, kept
at the present level, reduced or ended altogether? Programs to provide better and
faster mass transportation systems in and between metropolitan areas, such as
buses, trains, and in some cities, subways? (1 = increased, 0 = reduced, kept at
present level, or ended, NA = don't know)

(*Cont.*)

	Year	Institution	Roper ID

6   1976   Roper Organization   USRPRR1976-01
Turning now to the business of the country – we are faced with many problems in this country, none of which can be solved easily or inexpensively. I'm going to name some of these problems, and for each one I'd like you to tell me whether you think we're spending too much money on it, too little money, or about the right amount ... Improving public transportation. Too much, too little, about right, or don't know? (1 = too little, 0 = too much or about right, else coded NA)

7   1976   Roper Organization   USRPRR1976-02
Let's turn now to the question of public transportation. I'm going to name some different methods of transportation, and for each one would you tell me whether you think it is something that should get more financial support than it's getting, less support, or has about the right amount of support now. ... City bus and subway systems. (1 = more support, 0 = less support or about right, NA = don't know)

8   1976   Time Magazine   USYANK1976-8460
There's a lot of talk these days about cutting back on government spending. How do you feel – would you like to see the government spend more money, less money, or just about what they are spending now on: Mass transit (1 = more, 0 = less or the same, NA = not sure)

9   1977   Roper Organization   USRPRR1977-01
Turning now to the business of the country – we are faced with many problems in this country, none of which can be solved easily or inexpensively. I'm going to name some of these problems, and for each one I'd like you to tell me whether you think we're spending too much money on it, too little money, or about the right amount ... Improving public transportation. Too much, too little, about right, or don't know? (1 = too little, 0 = too much or about right, else coded NA)

10   1977   *Time Magazine*   USYANK1977-7610
President Carter's energy plan emphasizes certain things and not others. Will you tell me for each of the following whether you feel that President Carter's plan places too much emphasis on that policy, too little emphasis or about the right emphasis. How about: Doing something about public transportation (1 = too little emphasis, 0 = too much emphasis or right emphesis, NA = not sure)

11   1978   Roper Organization   USRPRR1978-01
Turning now to the business of the country – we are faced with many problems in this country, none of which can be solved easily or inexpensively. I'm going to name some of these problems, and for each one I'd like you to tell me whether you think we're spending too much money on it, too little money, or about the right amount ... Improving public transportation. Too much, too little, about right, or don't know? (1 = too little, 0 = too much or about right, else coded NA)

12   1978   Roper Organization   USRPRR1978-02
Let's turn now to the question of public transportation. I'm going to name some different methods of transportation, and for each one would you tell me whether you think it is something that should get more financial support than it's getting, less support, or has about the right amount of support now. ... City bus and subway systems. (1 = more support, 0 = less support or about right, NA = don't know)

(*Cont.*)

	Year	Institution	Roper ID

13   1979   Roper Organization   USRPRR1979-01

Turning now to the business of the country – we are faced with many problems in this country, none of which can be solved easily or inexpensively. I'm going to name some of these problems, and for each one I'd like you to tell me whether you think we're spending too much money on it, too little money, or about the right amount ... Improving public transportation. Too much, too little, about right, or don't know? (1 = too little, 0 = too much or about right, else coded NA)

14   1979   Roper Organization   USRPRR1979-03

Regardless of how you feel about the overall amount in the budget, you may think we should spend more or less on certain items. Here is a list of the major items in the budget. Would you go down that list and for each one tell me whether you think we should be spending more than President Carter has proposed in his budget, or spending less than he has proposed, or that he has proposed spending about the right amount on it? ... Improving public transportation.

15   1979   Roper Organization   USRPRR1979-05

I'd like to read you some of the points and proposals President Carter made and ask you for each whether you agree or disagree with him. President Carterproposed that some of the money from the windfall profits tax be used to build or improve mass transit systems. (1 = agree, 0 = disagree, NA = don't know

16   1980   Roper Organization   USRPRR1980-01

Turning now to the business of the country – we are faced with many problems in this country, none of which can be solved easily or inexpensively. I'm going to name some of these problems, and for each one I'd like you to tell me whether you think we're spending too much money on it, too little money, or about the right amount ... Improving public transportation. Too much, too little, about right, or don't know? (1 = too little, 0 = too much or about right, else coded NA)

17   1980   Roper Organization   USRPRR1980-02

Let's turn now to the question of public transportation. I'm going to name some different methods of transportation, and for each one would you tell me whether you think it is something that should get more financial support than it's getting, less support, or has about the right amount of support now. ... City bus and subway systems. (1 = more support, 0 = less support or about right, NA = don't know)

18   1981   NBC News/ Associated Press   USNBCAP1981-APRIL

Do you approve or disapprove of Reagan's proposal to cut federal funding for buses, subways, and other forms of mass transit? (among those who claim to have read/heard about President Reagan's economic proposals) (1 = disapprove, 0 = approve, NA = no opinion/not sure)

19   1981   Roper Organization   USRPRR1981-01

Turning now to the business of the country – we are faced with many problems in this country, none of which can be solved easily or inexpensively. I'm going to name some of these problems, and for each one I'd like you to tell me whether you think we're spending too much money on it, too little money, or about the right amount ... Improving public transportation. Too much, too little, about right, or don't know? (1 = too little, 0 = too much or about right, else coded NA)

(*Cont.*)

	Year	Institution	Roper ID

20 1981 Roper Organization USRPRR1981-04
President Reagan's economic plan calls mostly for cuts in federal government spending and for cuts in taxes. We'd like to ask you about the specific steps Reagan has proposed. Here are the major steps he has proposed. Would you tell me for each one whether you think it is something that should be done, or something that should not be done? ... Cut spending on aid to cities for mass transit. (1 = should not be done, 0 = should be done or have mixed feelings, NA = don't know)

21 1982 Roper Organization USRPRR1982-01
Turning now to the business of the country – we are faced with many problems in this country, none of which can be solved easily or inexpensively. I'm going to name some of these problems, and for each one I'd like you to tell me whether you think we're spending too much money on it, too little money, or about the right amount ... Improving public transportation. Too much, too little, about right, or don't know? (1 = too little, 0 = too much or about right, else coded NA)

22 1983 Roper Organization USRPRR1983-01
Turning now to the business of the country – we are faced with many problems in this country, none of which can be solved easily or inexpensively. I'm going to name some of these problems, and for each one I'd like you to tell me whether you think we're spending too much money on it, too little money, or about the right amount ... Improving public transportation. Too much, too little, about right, or don't know? (1 = too little, 0 = too much or about right, else coded NA)

23 1984 Roper Organization USRPRR1984-01
Turning now to the business of the country – we are faced with many problems in this country, none of which can be solved easily or inexpensively. I'm going to name some of these problems, and for each one I'd like you to tell me whether you think we're spending too much money on it, too little money, or about the right amount ... Improving public transportation. Too much, too little, about right, or don't know? (1 = too little, 0 = too much or about right, else coded NA)

24 1984 Roper Organization USRPRR1984-08
There are a number of things that have changed rather drastically over the past 20 years. Here is a list of some of them. Would you read down that list and for each one tell me whether you'd like to see continued advances and developments on it in the future, or whether you think we've gone as far as we should on it now, or whether we've already gone too far on it now. ... Methods of local public transportation (buses, subways, etc.) (1 = would like continued advances, 0 = gone as far as we should or too far, NA = don't know)

25 1985 Roper Organization USRPRR1985-01
Turning now to the business of the country – we are faced with many problems in this country, none of which can be solved easily or inexpensively. I'm going to name some of these problems, and for each one I'd like you to tell me whether you think we're spending too much money on it, too little money, or about the right amount ... Improving public transportation. Too much, too little, about right, or don't know? (1 = too little, 0 = too much or about right, else coded NA)

(Cont.)

	Year	Institution	Roper ID

26   1986   *Los Angeles Times*   USLAT1986-103
Congress will probably make some changes to the Reagan budget. We'd like to
know how you feel about some of the items. Of course, nobody wants to give up
necessary government services but, assuming that federal expenses for next year
will have to be cut, would you favor the elimination of federal support for Amtrak
and for urban mass transit, or would you rather consider some other way to cut
government expenses, instead? (1 = some other way, 0 = cuts to Amtrak and urban
mass transit, NA = not sure)

27   1986   NBC News/*Wall Street Journal*   USNBCWSJ1986-FEB
To help reduce the federal budget deficit, would you favor the elimination of
federal aid to build and help run local mass transit systems, or not? (1 = oppose
cuts, 0 = favor cuts, NA = not sure)

28   1986   Roper Organization   USRPRR1986-01
Turning now to the business of the country – we are faced with many problems
in this country, none of which can be solved easily or inexpensively. I'm going to
name some of these problems, and for each one I'd like you to tell me whether you
think we're spending too much money on it, too little money, or about the right
amount ... Improving public transportation. Too much, too little, about right, or
don't know? (1 = too little, 0 = too much or about right, else coded NA)

29   1987   Roper Organization   USRPRR1987-01
Turning now to the business of the country – we are faced with many problems
in this country, none of which can be solved easily or inexpensively. I'm going to
name some of these problems, and for each one I'd like you to tell me whether you
think we're spending too much money on it, too little money, or about the right
amount ... Improving public transportation. Too much, too little, about right, or
don't know? (1 = too little, 0 = too much or about right, else coded NA)

30   1995   *Time Magazine* and Cable   USYANK1995-95010
            News Network
I'm going to read you a list of programs that some people have suggested be
cut to balance the budget by the year 2002. For each, please tell me if it is
more important to make significant cuts in that program to balance the budget
or whether you think it is more important to prevent that program from being
significantly cut. Subsidies for buses, subways and other forms of mass transit.
(1 = prevent cuts, 0 = significant cuts, NA = not sure)

31   2004   Associated Press   USAP2004-06US2
Which do you think should be the higher priority for government spending?
Building more roads and highways or expanding public transportation such as
buses, subways, and trains? (1 = expanding public transportation such as buses,
subways and trains; 0 = building more roads and highways; NA = dont know)

32   2005   ABC News/*Time Magazine*/   USABCWASH2005-973
            Washington Post
For each item I name, please tell me how effective you think it is in easing traffic
congestion: very effective, somewhat effective, not so effective, or not effective at
all: Building or expanding public transportation (1 = very effective; 0 = somewhat
effective, not so effective, or not effective at all; NA = dont know/no opinion)

(*Cont.*)

Year	Institution	Roper ID

33   2006   Public Agenda Foundation   USPAF2006-LIB

I'm going to read a list of issues some communities are facing. For each one, considering what your local leaders need to deal with, please tell me how important of a priority it should be for be for your community. Do you think providing reliable public transportation should be a high, mid-level, or low priority for your community? (1 = high priority, 0 = mid-level or low priority, NA = dont know/refused)

34   2009   Planet Forward   USPAF2009-ENERGY

Do you favor or oppose each of the following energy-related proposals? Spending more tax money on public transportation such as bus and rail systems (1 = strongly favor; 0 = somewhat favor, somewhat oppose, or strongly oppose; NA = dont know/refused)

35   2010   Cable News Network   USORCCNN2010-001

Now I am going to read you a few provisions in that bill. For each one, please tell me whether you approve or disapprove of the use of federal funds for each one: Increased spending on trains, buses and other forms of mass transit (1 = approve, 0 = disapprove, NA = dont know/undecided/refused)

37   2014   ABC News / *Washington Post*   USABCWASH2014-1162

In general, do you think government efforts to reduce traffic congestion around the country should be focused more on expanding and building roads, or on providing more public transportation options, such as trains or buses? (1 = more public transportation options, 0 = building and expanding roads, NA = don't know/no opinion)

Survey Questions Used in Historical Highway Analysis

Number	Year	Institution	RoperID

1   1952   Gallup Organization   USAIPO1952-0492

Would you favor or oppose building one or two new super-highways across this state, to be paid for by special toll or charge on every car and truck using them? (1 = favor, 0 = oppose, NA = no opinion)

2   1953   Gallup Organization   USAIPO1953-0513

It has been proposed that two super-highways should be built across the country from east to west and two more from north to south. The cost would be paid by drivers who use the highways at the rate of about 1 cent per mile. Would you approve or disapprove of building these 4 toll highways? (1 = approve, 0 = disapprove, NA = no opinion)

3   1954   Gallup Organization   USAIPO1954-0527

It has been proposed that two super-highways should be built across the country from east to west and two more from north to south. The cost would be paid by drivers who use the highways at the rate of about 1 cent per mile. Would you approve or disapprove of building these four toll highways? (1 = approve, 0 = disapprove, NA = no opinion)

(*Cont.*)

Number	Year	Institution	RoperID
4	1956	Gallup Organization	USAIPO1956-0563

Do you think there is a need for building more express or super highways between the large cities of our country? (1 = yes, 0 = no, NA = don't know)

5	1974	Roper Organization	USRPRR1974-02

Let's turn now to the question of public transportation. I'm going to name some different methods of transportation, and for each one would you tell me whether you think it is something that should get more financial support than it's getting, less support, or has about the right amount of support now ... Interstate highway construction and improvement (1 = more support, 0 = less support or about right, NA = don't know)

6	1976	Roper Organization	USRPRR1976-02

Let's turn now to the question of public transportation. I'm going to name some different methods of transportation, and for each one would you tell me whether you think it is something that should get more financial support than it's getting, less support, or has about the right amount of support now ... Interstate highway construction and improvement (1 = more support, 0 = less support or about right, NA = don't know)

7	1978	Chicago Council on Foreign Relations	USAIPOSPGO1978-78175G

I am going to read a list of present federal government programs. For each, I'd like you to tell me whether you feel it should be expanded, cut back or kept about the same. ... Highway expenditures (1 = expand, 0 = cut back or keep the same, NA = not sure)

8	1978	Roper Organization	USRPRR1978-02

Let's turn now to the question of public transportation. I'm going to name some different methods of transportation, and for each one would you tell me whether you think it is something that should get more financial support than it's getting, less support, or has about the right amount of support now ... Interstate highway construction and improvement (1 = more support, 0 = less support or about right, NA = don't know)

9	1980	Roper Organization	USRPRR1980-02

Let's turn now to the question of public transportation. I'm going to name some different methods of transportation, and for each one would you tell me whether you think it is something that should get more financial support than it's getting, less support, or has about the right amount of support now ... Interstate highway construction and improvement (1 = more support, 0 = less support or about right, NA = don't know)

10	1981	Roper Organization	USRPRR1981-04

President Reagan's economic plan calls mostly for cuts in federal government spending and for cuts in taxes. We'd like to ask you about the specific steps Reagan has proposed. Here are the major steps he has proposed. [Card shown respondent] Would you tell me for each one whether you think it is something that should be done, or something that should not be done? ... Cut spending on aid to local governments for highways. (1 = should be done, 0 = should not be done or have mixed feelings, NA = don't know)

(*Cont.*)

Number	Year	Institution	RoperID
11	1982	Roper Organization	USRPRR1982-02

Let's turn now to the question of public transportation. I'm going to name some different methods of transportation, and for each one would you tell me whether you think it is something that should get more financial support than it's getting, less support, or has about the right amount of support now? First, interstate highway construction and improvement. Is that something that should get more financial support, less support, or does it have about the right amount now? (1 = more support, 0 = less support or about right, NA = don't know)

| 12 | 1982 | Roper Organization | USRPRR1982-07 |

Here are some things that have been reported in the news recently. Would you read down that list, and tell me how personally concerned you are about each of those reports – very concerned, somewhat concerned, not very concerned, or not at all concerned? ... Reports of the deterioration of our national highways. (1 = very concerned, 0 = somewhat, not very, or not at all concerned, NA = don't know)

| 13 | 1983 | Roper Organization | USRPRR1983-08 |

Here are some things that have been reported in the news recently. Would you read down that list, and tell me how personally concerned you are about each of those reports – very concerned, somewhat concerned, not very concerned, or not at all concerned? ... Reports of the deterioration of our national highways. (1 = very concerned, 0 = somewhat, not very, or not at all concerned, NA = don't know)

| 14 | 1984 | Roper Organization | USRPRR1984-06 |

There are many problems facing our nation today. But at certain times some things are more important than others, and need more attention from our federal government than others. I'd like to know for each of the things on this list whether you think it is something that government should be making a major effort on now, or something the government should be make some effort on now, or something not needing any particular government effort now. ... Taking steps to rebuild our federal highways and bridges. (1 = major effort, 0 = some or no particular effort, NA = don't know)

| 15 | 1988 | CBS News and *New York Times* | USCBSNYT1988-8807 |

Do you think federal spending onrepairing and maintaining highways and bridges ... should be increased, decreased, or kept the same? (1 = increased, 0 = decreased or kept the same, NA = don't know)

| 16 | 1990 | Times Mirror Center for the People & the Press | USTM1990-PS0590 |

If you had a say in making up the federal budget this year, for which of the following programs would you like to see spending increased, for which would you like to see spending decreased, or for which should spending be kept the same? Rebuilding highways, bridges, and roads. (1 = increased, 0 = decreased or kept the same, NA = dont know)

(*Cont.*)

Number	Year	Institution	RoperID
17	1992	*Time Magazine* and Cable News Network	USYANK1992-45438

Do you favor or oppose each of the following measures to spur the economy? Increasing funding for highways, roads, and bridges. (1 = favor, 0 = oppose, NA = not sure)

| 18 | 1994 | NBC News and *Wall Street Journal* | USNBCWSJ1994-4045 |

As President Clinton prepares to deliver his State of the Union address, there are many important issues facing the country. Let me read you a list of some of these issues and, for each one, please tell me if you think this should be an absolute priority for the Clinton Administration and this year's Congress or something that can be delayed until next year. Do you think this issue should be an absolute priority for the Clinton Administration and this year's Congress, or is this something that can be delayed until next year? Rebuilding the nation's highways and bridges. (1 = priority, 0 = not a priority, NA = not sure)

| 19 | 1998 | Cable News Network and *USA Today* | USAIPOCNUS1998-9801001 |

Now we have some more specific questions about what the government should do with a budget surplus. As I read a list of various proposals, please say whether you think each one should be a top priority for using the surplus, a high priority, a low priority, or not a priority at all. Increasing spending on highway construction (1 = top or high priority, 0 = low priority or not a priority, NA = don't know or refused)

| 20 | 1998 | UBS | USAIPOUBS1998-INVEST03 |

Now we have some more specific questions about what the government should do with a budget surplus. As I read a list of various proposals, please say whether you think each one should be a top priority for using the surplus, a high priority, a low priority, or not a priority at all. Increasing spending on highway construction (1 = top or high priority, 0 = low priority or not a priority, NA = don't know or refused)

| 21 | 1998 | *Time Magazine* and Cable News Network | USYANK1998-98001 |

As you may know, some economists expect that there will be a federal budget surplus in 1999 – that the government in Washington will collect more money in taxes than it is committed to spend for current government programs. Here are some proposals about how to spend some of the budget surplus. As I read each, please tell me whether you think that proposal should be a top priority for using some of the budget surplus, a high priority, a low priority, or not a priority at all. Increasing spending on federal highway programs (1 = top or high priority, 0 = low priority or not a priority, NA = dont know)

(*Cont.*)

Number	Year	Institution	RoperID
22	1999	Pew Research Center for the People & the Press	USPEW1999-MILLENNIUM

I'm going to read a list of some changes that have taken place over the last 100 years. Please tell me if you think each one has been a change for the better, a change for the worse, or hasnt made much difference. Has the Interstate highway system been a change for the better, a change for the worse, or hasn't made much difference? (1 = change for the better, 0 = change for the worse or not much difference)

| 23 | 2004 | Associated Press | USAP2004-06US2 |

Which do you think should be the higher priority for government spending? Building more roads and highways or expanding public transportation such as buses, subways, and trains? (1 = building more roads and highways; 0 = expanding public transportation such as buses, subways, and trains; NA = dont know)

| 24 | 2014 | ABC News/*Washington Post* | USABCWASH2014-1162 |

In general, do you think government efforts to reduce traffic congestion around the country should be focused more on expanding and building roads, or on providing more public transportation options, such as trains or buses? (1 = expanding and building roads, 0 = more public transportation options, NA = don't know/no opinion)

| 25 | 1992 | CBS News and *New York Times* | USCBSNYT1992-JAN92C |

Should federal spending on rebuilding and maintaining roads and bridges be increased, decreased, or kept the same? (1 = increased, 0 = decreased or kept the same, NA = don't know)

| 26 | 2000 | National Conference for Community and Justice | USPSRA2000-NCCJ |

The country faces many problems and the government has to concentrate its efforts on certain problems and give less attention to others. I'll mention several concerns and ask whether you believe each should be given top priority, above average but not top priority, average priority, or below average priority. Improving roads and bridges ... should this be given top priority, above average but not top priority, average priority, or below average priority? (1 = top priority; 0 = above average, avereage, or below average priority; NA = don't know)

| 27 | 2007 | CBS News | USCBS2007-08A |

Should federal spending on rebuilding and maintaining roads and bridges be increased, decreased, or kept the same? (1 = increased, 0 = decreased or kept the same, NA = don't know)

| 28 | 2008 | *USA Today* | USAIPOUSA2008-07 |

Regardless of whether you think an economic stimulus package should be passed, do you favor or oppose each of the following proposals? How about ... increasing government spending on US (United States) infrastructure such as roads and bridges? (1 = favor, 0 = oppose, NA = no opinion)

(Cont.)

Number	Year	Institution	RoperID
29	2008	Pew Research Center for the People & the Press	USPEW2008-12POL

As you may know, the government is considering several other proposals to address economic problems facing the nation. Do you think it is the right thing or the wrong thing for the government to spend billions of dollars ... to substantially increase spending on roads, bridges, and other public works projects? (1 = right thing, 0 = wrong thing, NA = don't know/ refused)

| 30 | 2009 | NBC News and *Wall Street Journal* | USNBCWSJ2009-6092 |

Now I would like to read you several parts of the economy stimulus legislation that is designed to help deal with the current economic recession. For each element, please tell me whether it is a good idea or a bad idea. ... Creating jobs through building or repairing roads and bridges (1 = good idea, 0 = bad idea, NA = not sure)

| 31 | 2009 | Pew Research Center for the People & the Press | USPEW2009-03POL |

As you may know, the government has taken or is considering other steps to address economic problems facing the nation. Do you think it is the right thing or the wrong thing for the government to spend billions of dollars ... to substantially increase spending on roads, bridges, and other public works projects? (1 = right thing, 0 = wrong thing, NA = don't know/refused)

| 32 | 2009 | Pew Research Center for the People & the Press | USPEW2009-06POL |

As you may know, the federal government has taken several steps to address economic problems facing the nation. Do you approve or disapprove of the government spending billions of dollars ... to substantially increase spending on roads, bridges, and other public works projects? (1 = approve, 0 = disapprove, NA = don't know/refused)

| 33 | 2011 | CBS News and *New York Times* | USCBSNYT2011-01C |

If you had to choose one, which of the following domestic programs would you be willing to reduce in order to cut government spending – education, or roads, bridges and other infrastructure, or science and medical research, or aid to the unemployed and poor? (1 = not roads/bridges/other infrastructure, 0 = roads/bridges/other infrastructure, NA

| 34 | 2011 | Pew Research Center for the People & the Press | USPEW2011-02POL |

If you were making up the budget for the federal government this year (2011), would you increase spending, decrease spending or keep spending the same for ... rebuilding highways, bridges and roads? (1 = increase, 0 = decrease or keep the same, NA = don't know/refused)

(*Cont.*)

Number	Year	Institution	RoperID
35	2011	ABC News / *Washington Post*	USABCWASH2011-1121

Now thinking about budget problems at the state level. I'm going to name some proposals that may help reduce state budget deficits. For each, please tell me if that's something you would support strongly, support somewhat, oppose somewhat or oppose strongly in your state. How about ... reduce spending on roads and other infrastructure projects? (1 = oppose strongly; 0 = oppose somewhat, support somewhat, or support strongly)

Number	Year	Institution	RoperID
36	2011	NBC News and *Wall Street Journal*	USNBCWSJ2011-11382

President (Barack) Obama is expected to outline a jobs plan in the coming weeks. I'm going to read some different proposals that could be considered by the president. For each one please tell me if you think this proposal is a good idea, a bad idea, or do you not know enough about it to have an opinion. ... Funding a new road construction bill (1 = good idea, 0 = bad idea, NA = don't know enough)

Notes

1 On only a handful of occasions have transportation issues been mentioned by even one respondent on Gallup's Most Important Problem series, as assembled and coded by the Policy Agendas Project (2015).

2 Absent a natural experiment or policy experiment that randomly assigns people to different levels of reliance on a public policy, these two scenarios are observationally equivalent.

3 For example, the GSS transit and road spending items are more correlated with each other than with any other item.

4 For the highway study, search terms included "highway," "road," "freeway," and "expressway." For mass transit, search terms included "transit" and "mass transportation." Items that pertained to localized projects or asked only for an evaluation of conditions (e.g., the quality of roads) were excluded from the analysis.

5 Type of place, population density, and income were not included because they were not recorded consistently (if at all) across the diverse archived surveys.

6 All question text and documentation appears in the chapter appendix. Several of the questions from recent surveys presented choices between highways (or transit) and other alternatives.

7　While more data would be needed to test the idea, the Republican swing against transit might be attributed to increased elite Republican campaigning against transit and rail projects during the Obama years. President Obama's high-speed rail plans, for example, were strongly opposed by leading Republican governors, including Florida's Rick Scott and Wisconsin's Scott Walker. Engaged and attentive Republicans, especially, were likely to pick up these elite cues. Whether this shift against mass transit can also be tied to the racialized politics of the Obama years is also an open question (Tesler and Sears, 2010).

8　See Mummolo and Nall (2017) and the discussion of the conjoint analysis in Chapter 2 for additional details.

9　This is a generally accurate description of the federal transportation funding scheme.

10　Several items were included on the list that may never be seriously considered in transportation legislation. For example, providing debit cards (or vouchers) to the poor for transportation has been discussed in libertarian transportation circles (O'Toole, 2010), but adoption of such a policy is unlikely.

11　Zip-code data enabled the merging of respondent attitude data with 2010 Census zip-code tabulation area (ZCTA) shapefile data to construct respondents' context, including population density.

12　On the 2015 survey, low income was defined as less than $30,000 per year, middle income as $30,000–$80,000 per year, and high income as $80,000 per year and above. On the 2013 survey, the high-income category began at $85,000.

13　Such a policy is at odds with liberal transportation thinking, which proposes taxing driving and subsidizing transit.

14　Americans are likely unaware of the specific funding ratio, but this difference also suggests that the bipartisan maintenance of the policy in Congress is not supported by a bipartisan public.

15　While this idea was not outlined in full detail for survey respondents, the original idea presented in O'Toole (2010) was a proposal to eliminate transit subsidies and effectively privatize transportation assistance for the poor.

16　See, for example, partisan gaps on the GSS spending item for "welfare" versus transportation items (Nall, Agrawal, and Nixon, 2017).

17　By construction, this survey method will tend to induce greater partisan separation because of the head-to-head comparisons.

18　These tests do not include a multiple-testing adjustment.

5 | Implications for Transportation Policy Making

Previous chapters showed that highways have facilitated the urban–suburban sorting of American partisans across the postwar period. In the years since construction of the Interstate Highway System, the Republican Party has become increasingly suburban and rural. While Democrats have also suburbanized over the same period, they dominate central cities. I have shown that this likely has a substantial effect on how members of the two parties view transportation policy. Democrats and Republicans in the electorate are increasingly divided over policies that previously elicited bipartisan agreement. Whether this change has been due to conservatives and liberals geographically sorting, or a result of increasingly nonurban Republicans identifying their personal interests in the suburbs, attitudes on these issues are now tied to partisanship.

Do these changes matter to public policy? If American partisans are extending their coherent ideological views to transportation policy, we might expect them to influence institutions, from Congress to regional transportation planning organizations, that decide transportation policy. In this chapter, I examine the consequences of partisan geographic sorting for transportation policy. If, as Chapter 4 suggests, Democrats and Republicans increasingly disagree over transportation policy, and split along urban–suburban lines, under what circumstances will this lead to policies that worsen spatial inequality?

While this chapter is far more exploratory than previous chapters, the results here collectively demonstrate the importance of partisan geographic polarization in the setting of transportation policy. The findings in this chapter suggest that partisan geographic polarization has mattered to transportation policy more in a local than in a national context. The mere presence of partisan geographic polarization and growing partisan attitudinal differences does not imply that policy conflict will increase across geographic levels.

At the federal level, the urban–suburban divide has seemed to have little effect on longstanding transportation institutions, including the politically robust programs that fund highways and transit. Even as urban Republicans have vanished from Congress and conservative Republicans have introduced bills to cut federal mass transit funding – moves that reflect the general polarization of the two party caucuses – the transportation policy status quo has remained remarkably robust. Status quo bias and strong norms of universalism around transportation legislation (Panagopoulos and Schank, 2007), combined with a paucity of member bills on transportation issues, suggest that growing urban–suburban polarization has done little to change federal transportation policies. As a result, Congress can appear to be a "policy-free zone" when it comes to transportation issues (Panagopoulos and Schank, 2007, 178). The truth of this observation is corroborated by the prevalence of congressional institutions that favor compromise and a universalistic distribution of transportation projects, leading to ongoing bipartisan compromises on transportation legislation.

By contrast, clearly partisan – and urban–suburban – battle lines have formed over transportation policy at the metropolitan level. In addition to facilitating partisan geographic sorting, by devolving transportation programs to local and regional governments and agencies in recent decades, federal transportation policy has made metropolitan transportation outcomes more vulnerable to urban–suburban polarization.

I present three case studies that illustrate how urban–suburban polarization has had inconsistent effects at various levels of transportation policy making: on congressional transportation legislation, on metropolitan planning organizations (MPOs), and regional transit-financing referenda.

In the first case study, I examine how congressional transportation politics were initially defined by both partisan and place-based voting, with more urban liberals pursuing pro-transit legislation throughout the 1960s and 1970s. However, since the 1970s, the politics of transportation legislation have been marked by two features: a decline in the number of member-sponsored bills pertaining to either highways or transit, and, since the 1970s, typically incremental changes to the status quo. While many of the conflicts over transportation bills are now resolved in negotiations over large transportation bills, there is little evidence that the shifting geographic bases of the two parties have meaningfully changed legislation, as measured by member bill proposals. The robustness of the status quo appears to be rooted in the universalist norms that continue to surround omnibus transportation legislation. As I discuss, this universalism has manifested itself in a decades-long understanding that "highway" bills will deliver about 20 percent of funding to mass transportation programs.

I next present two quantitative case studies that address the consequences of devolution of transportation policy to the local level, and discuss how this devolution interacts with urban–suburban polarization.

I begin by examining the unintended consequences of the extension of additional project planning power to MPOs under the Intermodal Surface Transportation Efficiency Act of 1991 (ISTEA). The operating rules of MPOs have given disproportionate voting power to suburban jurisdictions. In a polarized metropolitan area, this may result in a more unequal distribution of program benefits by suburb-dominated MPO boards. Even in the absence of urban–suburban polarization, there is accumulating evidence that MPOs distribute the benefits of transportation projects to better represented communities. Because Republicans tend to be less supportive of urban transportation investments, geographic polarization combined with malapportioned board representation may result in unequal funding. In the second case study, I demonstrate that partisan geography also matters when questions are put directly to voters through county and regional transportation finance ballot measures, which typically take the form of so-called local option sales taxes (LOST), incremental property tax assessments, or bond measures. I examine two November 2016 ballot measures supporting public transit agencies in the San Francisco and Detroit areas. These metropolitan regions differ on multiple dimensions, including income, racial composition, population density, and transit utilization. Yet partisanship appears to dictate referendum vote choice in both metropolitan areas – so much so that voting on transit measures is almost as strongly partisan as votes for down-ballot partisan candidates. In addition to illustrating the policy consequences of metropolitan partisan geography, the results of these referenda strongly corroborate the survey results presented in Chapter 4. Partisan polarization, mediated through regional institutions, can undermine the provision of urban mobility.

The Minimal Effects of Geographic Polarization on Congressional Transportation Policy Making

Where should we expect to see measurable effects of geographic polarization on transportation policy? Given the considerable attention to congressional polarization (McCarty, Poole, and Rosenthal, 2006), Congress is the first place political scientists concerned with polarization might look to find such effects. We might expect the urban–suburban sorting of Democrats and Republicans will also influence the congressional politics of transportation policy, especially on matters pertaining to investments in urban mass transportation. However, evidence for such polarization is scarce. Until the 1970s, urban transportation policy was a more uncertain and contested issue domain. As commercial passenger railroads and private transit operators went out of business and were replaced by public transit agencies, congressional legislation aiming to subsidize urban mass transportation and passenger railroads proliferated in the early 1960s. This matter became largely settled after the Federal-Aid Highway Act of 1973, which allowed states to divert unused Highway Trust Fund dollars to transit for the first time. While this provision would later be formalized with the creation of a transit-specific account in the highway trust fund, the Federal Aid Highway Act initiated a tradition of devoting about 20 percent of transportation outlays to transit in the years ahead (Congressional Budget Office, 2015). Likely as a result of this persistent grand bargain, few transit- or highway-specific bills have been introduced by members of either party since the late 1970s.

At the time of this writing, one might expect future congressional controversies over transportation to be shaped by urban–suburban partisan polarization. The two parties in Congress have become more ideologically coherent and disciplined (McCarty, Poole, and Rosenthal, 2006). Over the same period, Democratic and Republican representatives have increasingly segregated along urban–rural lines. Rural House Democrats are a rarity, while urban Republicans, never a substantial presence in Congress, have almost entirely disappeared in the last two decades. Moreover, the decline of urban representation has been asymmetric, consistent with the asymmetric suburbanization of the two parties. While many House Democrats represent a large city, urban representatives retained a fairly steady minority share of the Democratic caucus in recent decades. The top panel of Figure 5.1 displays the development of the average population density of congressional districts of the two party caucuses since 1980. As the bottom panel of Figure 5.1 shows, the proportion of Republicans representing the densest districts (over 10,000 persons per square mile, approximately the same population density as the District of Columbia) has shrunk from around 5 percent of all Republican House districts to none. Meanwhile, the proportion of House Democrats representing such high-density districts varied but remained consistently higher than the Republicans' urban share since the 80th Congress (1948).

Two sets of expectations might be drawn from Figure 5.1. First, if we believe that representatives are election-minded, we should expect to find that Republicans sponsored little legislation addressing urban transportation needs (Freemark, 2011). Second, the small proportion of representatives from large cities even in the Democratic Party means that bloc voting by urban representatives will never be sufficient to protect federal funding for urban transportation needs. Urban interests hoping to extract transportation investments from Congress will need to compromise and extract concessions from the large majority of Congress that represents suburban and rural districts. (I will not address here whether the urban–suburban polarization examined in previous chapters is actually affecting the urban and nonurban makeup of the Democratic and Republican parties. It is sufficient to say that urban–suburban polarization has grown concurrently with polarization in Congress.)

Without attempting to draw an ironclad causal link, we can nevertheless establish whether congressional behavior around urban transportation issues is changing accordingly. To do so, I examine bill introductions by members of the House of Representatives. Why examine these, as opposed to roll call votes? One reason is that transportation bills typically pass by large margins, frequently after being stuffed with pork-barrel projects to win broad support for the full bill (Evans, 1994, 2004; Lee, 2003). By contrast, bills introduced by members of Congress can shed additional light on members' policy preferences. Even when the bills are introduced for public attention and are not sincere proposals, they may be understood as an expressive act meant to appeal to member constituencies concerned about the policy issue (Mayhew, 2002). I examine bill-introduction data from

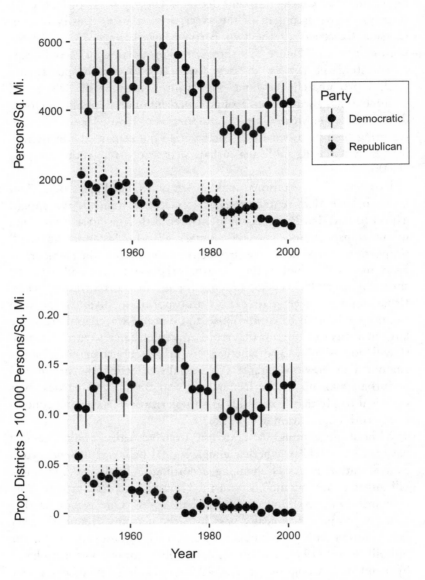

Figure 5.1. Changes in average House district population density and representation of population-dense districts (over 10,000 persons per square mile), by party, 1947 to 2003. Ninety-five percent confidence intervals accompany the values for each Congress. Sources: Adler (2014) and Lewis et al. (2017).

the Congressional Bills Project (Adler and Wilkerson, 2015), which collected information on bills proposed from the 80th Congress (1947–1949) to the 114th Congress (2013–2015). In addition to providing a comprehensive list of introduced bills by bill number (along with data on the introducing member), the database includes a bill issue area and a bill title useful for categorizing the legislation. The database also includes supplementary information on each bill, including the first and second dimensions of the proposer's DW-NOMINATE score, a widely used roll call-based measure that captures members' left–right ideology. With additional information on the bill author's district and other member characteristics (Adler, 2014), we can establish whether growing urban–suburban polarization has had a discernable effect on the types of transportation legislation introduced by House members.

To create a set of bills related to highways and transit from the Adler–Wilkerson data, two research assistants identified all bills that Adler and Wilkerson (2015) categorized as such. To filter the bills to include only those relevant to transportation, the bill descriptions were text-searched for terms related to highways and mass transit.[1] Bills were coded as belonging to one of five categories, the most important of which were bills that authorized or appropriated funding for programs to deliver transportation services:[2]

- Bureaucratic: Bills that create or reorganize a government agency.
- Research: Bills authorizing or appropriating funding for research programs and institutes. (These programs often appear to be pork-barrel projects.)
- Revenue: Bills primarily or exclusively dedicated to raising revenue. For example, the Highway Revenue Act of 1956 established a new gasoline tax that became the primary funding source for the Highway Trust Fund.
- Appropriation or authorization bills for transportation outlays: bills directly favoring transportation construction programs, individual projects, or subsidies. This type of bill was of primary interest in the analysis presented here. For example, the Federal Aid Highway Act of 1956 authorized the Interstate Highway System and directed a 90 percent federal match to the states to facilitate construction. This category also includes proposals for tax expenditure programs, such as those providing for commuter-related tax deductions.

The primary items of interest were bills to support transportation programs of general or national benefit. Within each of the preceding categories, bills were further categorized according to the following scheme:

- Particularistic versus general: A bill was deemed particularistic if it was written to deliver benefits to a delimited geographic area, and was deemed general if not. For example, a bill specifically assigned to fund a bridge in a member's district was deemed particularistic and not included in the final data set.[3]
- Urban versus rural preference: This refers to a bill whose title or description indicated targeted benefits to either urban or rural places (or residents thereof). A bill was only coded as "urban" or "rural" if the purpose of the legislation was general, as opposed to particularistic. (This level of specificity was rarely provided in bill titles and was not deemed useful in analysis.)

The only bills retained were those coded exclusively as transit-related or highway-related, but not both, and that delivered general benefits.

With increasing geographic polarization over time, we might have expected to see more pro-highway and fewer transit bills coming from the increasingly conservative and nonurban Republican caucus, while urban representatives would, compared to Republicans, introduce relatively more transit and fewer highway bills over time. I find little support for this idea. We might also expect more transit bills to have come from more liberal (usually urban) districts. Figures 5.2 and 5.3 display the changing ideological makeup of the party caucuses and median member, as well as the ideology of highway and transit bill introducers over time, as captured by the first-dimension DW-NOMINATE score. As can be seen in the graphs, support for transit funding has long been associated with left ideology. The horizontal axis of each graph displays the Congress, starting with the 80th Congress (1947–1948), while the vertical axis displays the ideological ideal-point score. The solid lines in each graph represent, top to bottom, the Republican caucus, chamber, and Democratic medians in the House, while the fitted lowess curves represent the average DW-NOMINATE first-dimension scores of bill proposers in each party.

The first, and most obvious, fact conveyed by the figures is that both transit and highway bills were far more abundant as Congress was engaged with urban transportation problems in the first few postwar

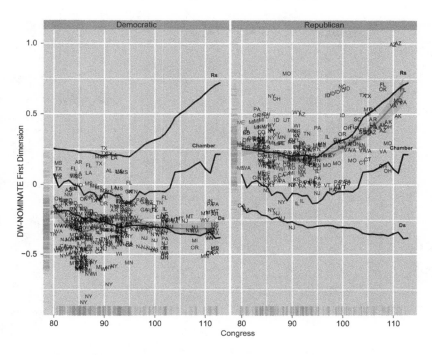

Figure 5.2. Introduction of general highway-only bills in the House by party, ideology (DW-NOMINATE score), and member state. Each data point represents a single bill proposal from a member representing a district in the listed state. For reference, party and chamber medians appear as solid lines. Sources: Adler (2014); Adler and Wilkerson (2015).

decades. Members introduced numerous highway bills across this period, while transit-related bills began appearing in large numbers starting in the early 1960s. In addition, bill introductions have tended to be consistent with the partisan and ideological bases of support for transportation policy already revealed in public opinion data. Highway bills originated from both parties, and from across the ideological and geographic range of each party caucus. As a result, the ideology of highway bill introducers has tended to closely match each party's median over time. Transit bill introducers, by contrast, has been consistently to the left of the chamber and their respective party medians. Transit bills have tended to come from representatives serving transit-heavy states, including New York, New Jersey, and California.

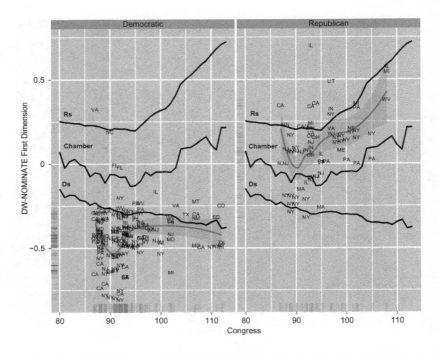

Figure 5.3. Introduction of general transit-only bills in the House by party, ideology (DW-NOMINATE score), and member state. Each data point represents a single bill proposal from a member representing a district in the listed state. For reference, party and chamber medians appear as solid lines. Sources: Adler (2014); Adler and Wilkerson (2015).

To establish whether urban–suburban geographic polarization has changed the origins of bill proposals over time, I examine transit and highway bill introductions as a function of member economic ideology (first-dimension DW-NOMINATE score), party, and population density. I group the data into four periods: 1961–1970, 1971–1980, 1981–1990, and 1990–2014. These decades roughly capture four eras in the post-Interstate debate over highway and transit funding: the early years of federal investment in transit, the gradual development of transit as an alternative to highways and as a response to the oil price shocks of the 1970s, the Reagan era (with an attendant threat of reduced transit subsidies), and a current era in which transit has become well established as part of a regular transportation bill (Altshuler and Luberoff, 2003, ch. 2).

For each of these periods, I regressed indicators of transit and highway bill sponsorship on member party and log population density. If interest in highway and transit legislation had been based on district population density or urban population share alone, we would expect to see a strong relationship between bill introduction and density, and little relationship to party (and vice versa). I also examined how introduction of highway and transit legislation varied with DW-NOMINATE score, separately for urban Democrats, nonurban Democrats, urban Republicans, and nonurban Republicans. I fitted a logistic regression to data points for each party and decade.[4]

The results of this analysis indicate that partisanship and geography both appeared to explain bill proposals in the 1960s and 1970s. One might have expected a clearer divergence between the two parties over time, but such a difference has either been absent or difficult to detect, mostly because both party caucuses have produced fewer highway- or transit-specific bills.

In the case of highway legislation, members from both parties and from cities with varying population density levels have introduced bills. However, 1970s antihighway protests and conservation concerns around the time of the 1973 Arab oil embargo may have led predominantly Democratic urban representatives not to introduce as much pro-highway legislation. In the 1970s, among representatives from both parties, there was a negative and statistically significant effect of district population density on introduction of highway legislation. About 10 to 15 percent of representatives from all districts, but barely any representatives from the most dense districts, introduced highway legislation during the decade. However, House members of both parties were unlikely to introduce highway legislation in the 1980s and 1990s, regardless of their district population density (Figure 5.4).

An temporally similar pattern occurred around mass transit legislation (Figure 5.5). Between 1961 and 1970, Republicans were less likely than Democrats to hail from high-density districts, but the few urban Republicans were somewhat more likely than urban Democrats to introduce transit legislation. By the 1970s, Republicans and Democrats representing districts with the same population densities were about equally likely to introduce transit bills. Ironically, perhaps because transit advocates won a diversion of transit funding from the Highway Trust Fund in 1973 and consolidated those gains under the Surface Transportation Assistance Act of 1982 (which

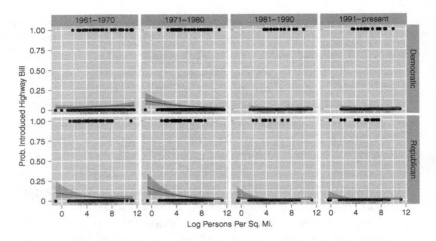

Figure 5.4. Predicted probability of a member introducing a highway-specific bill in a Congress, by decade, member party, and district density. Sources: Adler (2014); Adler and Wilkerson (2015).

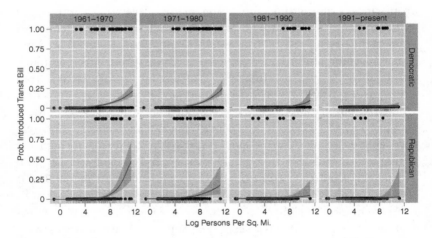

Figure 5.5. Predicted probability of a member introducing a transit-specific bill in a Congress by decade, member party, and district density. Sources: Adler (2014); Adler and Wilkerson (2015).

dedicated a fixed share of gas tax proceeds to mass transit), by the 1980s and 1990s few representatives from either party were introducing specific transit legislation. That is, the protransit policy entrepreneurship was a victim of its own success.[5]

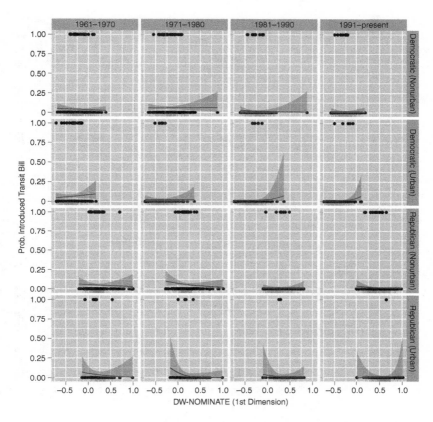

Figure 5.6. Predicted probability of a member introducing a highway-specific bill in a Congress, by decade, member party and large-city indicator, and first-dimension DW-NOMINATE score. Sources: Adler (2014); Adler and Wilkerson (2015).

Since more liberal House members have been more likely to come from more urban areas, we might expect population density and liberal ideology to be completely collinear. Figures 5.6 and 5.7, which present the probability that a member introduced a highway spending bill, provides limited support for this hypothesis. While the data suggest that density and urbanism influence whether a member of Congress introduces highway legislation, the results are insufficiently powered to be conclusive. No strong evidence exists one way or another to assess the role of geographic distribution of partisans in

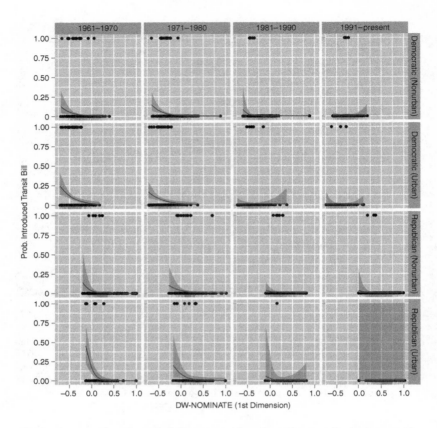

Figure 5.7. Predicted probability a member introduces a highway-specific bill in a Congress, by decade, member party and large-city indicator, and first-dimension DW-NOMINATE score. Sources: Adler (2014); Adler and Wilkerson (2015).

advocacy for highway and transit legislation. Ideology does appear to be tied to support for transit in both parties, but its effects were most apparent in the 1960s and 1970s. Given urban–suburban polarization and the increased association between party and place of residence, one might have expected to see more urban-related bills from Democrats and, if a policy feedback account is to believed, more pro-highway bills from nonurban Democrats and nonurban Republicans.[6] Instead, since the 1970s, the number of bills related to transit and highways has plummeted in both parties. As the House

Republican caucus has shifted far to the right, it has also become less urban. The few remaining urban Republican representatives in recent years have introduced no transit bills. However, neither have Democrats introduced transit-specific legislation since the 1980s.

One way of reading this result is that recent data are far too sparse to draw any meaningful conclusions. However, this sparseness is also indicative of how the politics of federal transportation policy have, in specific ways, changed dramatically since the 1960s and 1970s in ways that mitigate polarization's effects. Several factors help explain why it is hard to see the effect of urban–suburban polarization congressional politics: there is a mismatch between public opinion on transportation and the congressional institutions that manage transportation policy, party discipline obscures geographic effects, and centralizing institutions discourage policy entrepreneurship by individual members. One potential reason for the decline in open conflict on this issue is that urban mass transit advocates have become vested in supporting transit programs exclusively through the "highway bill" since the Federal-Aid Highway Act of 1973 supported transit through the Highway Trust Fund. Highway advocates can count on urban transit advocates and other proponents of transportation alternatives to support bills that are still dominated by highway spending in exchange for a share of the transportation budget.[7] Congressional norms, especially around the universalism and the surprisingly robust highway-transit logroll, can be expected to continue to dull polarization's effects on congressional transportation policy debates (Weingast, 1979, 1994).

Devolution Exposes Transportation Policy to Geographic Polarization

Urban–suburban polarization's seemingly minimal effect on congressional lawmaking may mean that weightier institutional factors outweigh geographic polarization – or just that Congress may be the wrong place to expect metropolitan geographic polarization to change transportation policy. Transportation may rarely bubble up as a contentious national policy issue, but major transportation policy controversies do arise locally. The devolution of transportation planning creates additional opportunities for geographic polarization to influence policy. When transportation decisions are devolved, local geographic polarization is likely to combine with local institutions to shape the implementation of transportation and other policies.[8] I present findings regarding two examples of local control and its vulnerability to local preferences: the granting of additional transportation planning authority to MPOs under the 1991 ISTEA transportation legislation (which reinforced the already strong American tradition of transportation policy devolution) and empowerment of local voters to fund or defund regional transit programs through referenda. ISTEA gave MPOs a formal role in the designation of transportation projects and planning in metropolitan areas. As part of the "devolution revolution," the new transportation law promised to improve the delivery of transportation programs to metropolitan areas by giving the organizations – which had been granted a toothless role in metropolitan-level planning and research under previous transportation legislation – greater control over the process. The hope, expressed by Sen. Daniel Patrick Moynihan (D-NY), Environment and Public Works Committee chair and ISTEA's primary legislative sponsor, was that empowering existing but underutilized organizations would better address uniquely metropolitan concerns that state highway departments had neglected as they neglected central cities to build Interstate highways (Dilger, 2011).[9] Under the recent reauthorization of transportation legislation under MAP-21, signed into law in 2012, approximately 29 percent of the appropriation given to each state was assigned to the Surface Transportation Fund, which, in turn, was suballocated to metropolitan areas for distribution according to MPO plans (Federal Highway Administration, 2015). Thus, MPOs control a de facto slush fund that they allocate across their jurisdictions.[10]

Giving more power to MPOs has shifted more control to the metropolitan level, subjecting decisions to local preferences (Gerber and Gibson, 2009). A great irony, if not an unintended consequence, of devolving responsibility to MPOs is that doing so has shifted decision-making from state transportation officials thought insufficiently attentive to metropolitan transportation concerns to boards that can be dominated by affluent and high-growth suburbs (Rose and Mohl, 2012, 174). Representation on MPO boards is typically assigned by jurisdiction rather than population (Sanchez, 2006), and MPO board members will often try to operate by consensus, delivering small and highly localized projects to member jurisdictions rather than undertaking regionwide transportation programs (Puentes, 2011). In addition, MPOs are not elected as legislatures and are not covered under the "one-person, one-vote" standard that applies to elected legislatures or boards of general-purpose governments (Lewis, 1998). Under this representational scheme, populous cities are usually underrepresented and disadvantaged.

Instead of strengthening urban communities' vote over metropolitan transportation issues, MPOs instead give suburban areas a disproportionately strong voice in metropolitan transportation planning. Of the forty-nine major MPOs in the lower forty-eight states, as of 2006, only sixteen provided for any form of population-based representation.[11] Unweighted voting rules lead to greater suburban overrepresentation, not because suburban areas typically constitute a minority of the metropolitan population, but because they are fractured into multiple jurisdictions.[12]

Sanchez (2006) examines the extent to which urban jurisdictions receive MPO board representation proportional to their populations. Figure 5.8 plots the proportion of seats that urban areas held on each board (vertical axis) against the voting power that urban areas *would have held* under population-weighted representation (horizontal axis). In MPO regions where urban areas constitute less than two-thirds of the metropolitan population, they typically hold only about one-quarter of unweighted MPO votes. Even in urban-dominated MPOs, urban areas remain underrepresented. Urban areas hold a majority of the population in twenty of the forty-nine MPOs appearing in the Sanchez (2006) sample, but under unweighted voting they hold majority voting power on only two boards.

The empowerment of MPOs and the underrepresentation of urban areas demonstrates the importance of urban–suburban polarization within individual metropolitan areas. The preceding analysis of MPO voting power indicates that if urban and suburban bloc voting occurs, urban areas are at a severe disadvantage. As transportation policy preferences become more tied to partisanship, MPOs that include more Republican suburbs may be expected to adopt policies reflecting Republican suburbanites' opposition to investment in central cities. However, in less polarized metropolitan areas with more suburban Democrats, suburban representatives on MPO boards might be expected to endorse projects benefiting central cities. Figure 5.9 displays the relationship between partisan geographic segregation, represented by the dissimilarity index in the 2008 precinct-level two-party presidential vote (Massey and Denton, 1988), and

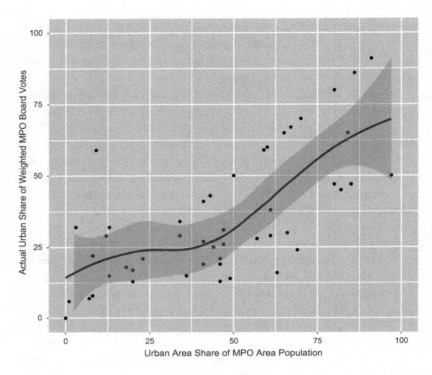

Figure 5.8. Urban share of MPO board votes versus urban share of MPO area population, 2004. Population-based voting weights (often adopted by MPOs on an ad hoc basis) are included in the analysis. Optional population-weighted voting is not usually applied, but is presented here to make conservative assumptions about representation levels. Source: Adapted from Sanchez (2006).

net suburban overrepresentation on MPOs (the difference between suburban jurisdictions' representation and their unweighted voting share). The dissimilarity index captures the extent to which Democrats and Republicans (measured here using the 2008 presidential two-party vote) are unevenly distributed across voting precincts. Polarization and suburban MPO overrepresentation under an unweighted voting rule are weakly correlated. However, Figure 5.9 shows that all but six MPOs out of forty-nine are biased in favor of the suburbs.[13]

Evidence of representational biases in MPOs is clear-cut. A more difficult and still open question is whether pro-suburban

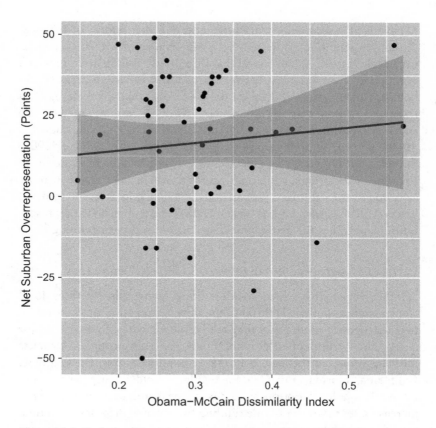

Figure 5.9. Relationship between segregation (measured by the Obama-McCain dissimilarity index) and suburban overrepresentation on MPOs. Pro-suburban bias in MPO voting power is widespread and positively, albeit weakly, correlated with metropolitan geographic polarization. Source: Sanchez (2006); Ansolabehere and Rodden (2012).

malapportionment in MPO boards, combined with urban–suburban polarization, leads to worse inequality in the distribution of projects by MPOs. Data that would allow us to answer this question on a national sample are not standardized, and the geographic distribution of projects is often tracked by MPOs only in terms of general categories. Even when looking at MPOs' published project lists, it is not always feasible to place projects in precise or bounded geographic locations.[14] However, multiple studies have found a link between

MPOs' representational procedures and the distribution of projects. Presenting tentative evidence on the importance of MPO representation, Nelson et al. (2004) found that three metropolitan areas in which voting was most balanced between urban and suburban areas (Puget Sound, Cincinnati, and Tampa) devoted about half of their budgets to transit (a primarily urban concern) while three dominated by the suburbs (Southeast Michigan, Rhode Island, and Nashville) devoted 80–90 percent of their funds to roads. Gerber and Gibson (2009) find that MPOs with more elected board members were more likely to support local versus regional projects, which may result in more advantages for suburban jurisdictions.[15] Finally, in a recent study of Texas MPO boards, An and Bostic (2017) show that board representation determines the geographic distribution of project funding.[16]

Partisan Geographic Polarization and Direct Democracy

Another means by which local political geography dictates local transportation politics is through the direct expression of voter transportation policy preferences through ballot measures. In several major states, the raising of additional funds for transportation projects must be approved through local tax or bond measures. For example, California, Florida, and Georgia regularly hold county or regional referenda on local option sales taxes, measures that incrementally increase sales taxes to provide funding for specific purposes, including transportation programs.[17] In Michigan, local governments are constitutionally required to seek approval for increased property tax rates, and local transit systems are often funded through property tax referenda. In other states, ballot measures are set up to approve general-obligation bonds to finance transportation infrastructure projects. The content of such referenda is usually set by county governments, regional transit authorities, or MPOs, which strategically draft such measures to win over the necessary winning coalition (which may be as large as a two-thirds majority). While referendum proposers therefore have strategic "first-mover" control over the policy options that come before voters (Romer and Rosenthal, 1979), referenda represent the most direct observational test of partisan geography's influence in regional transportation policy making.

Chapter 4 survey results suggest that partisanship will be linked to support for transportation referenda, but the level of support is likely to vary depending on the nature of the programs being funded.

Here, I focus on referenda in support of public transit agencies. Such agencies can be vulnerable to opposition from suburbs, especially when maintenance of a regional transit system is dependent on the voluntary participation of individual counties or other political jurisdictions within the an agency's service area. Under such circumstances, geographic polarization between urban and suburban areas may well determine the fate or viability of entire regional transportation projects and programs.[18]

I collected data from two widely publicized regional transit referenda, one in the Detroit metropolitan area and the other in the San Francisco area, both conducted concurrently with the 2016 presidential election. In Detroit, a measure to raise $4.6 billion in property taxes for Detroit's Regional Transit Authority (RTA) won only 49.5 percent of the vote, failing to win a majority in the politically balanced but highly polarized Detroit area (Fleming, 2016). The Detroit referendum was considered especially important to the future of mobility in the region because transit programs in the Detroit area had long been fragmented between the City of Detroit's transit system, the Detroit Department of Transportation (DDOT); and the exclusively suburban Southeastern Michigan Area Rapid Transit (SMART).[19] Republican Governor Rick Snyder created the RTA in 2012 to coordinate activities between the urban and suburban agencies, but did not endow it with state funding (Office of Governor Rick Snyder, 2012). The additional property tax proposed under the referendum would have provided funding for several new regional transportation infrastructure programs, including bus rapid transit (BRT) lines and new commuter rail service between Ann Arbor and Detroit. Bay Area Rapid Transit (BART) Measure RR, placed on the November 2016 ballot in BART's three-county service area (Alameda, Contra Costa, and San Francisco), was a $3.5 billion bond measure introduced by the independent transit authority's governing board to cover general system improvements and repairs. The measure won 70.1 percent of the vote, clearing the two-thirds vote required of such measures in California.[20] While many other counties and metropolitan areas conducted transit referenda in recent elections, I focus on these two as they are two major and different metropolitan areas seeking very large investments across multiple counties.

In order to capture the role of partisanship in transportation referenda, I assembled a GIS database of precinct-level election returns.

Election returns were obtained from county election officials. Where available, precinct-level shapefiles were obtained from county election officials, or from news media open-data projects.[21] The precinct-level records containing the referendum and two-party presidential vote were merged with American Community Survey (ACS) data to assess the extent to which partisan voting is merely proxying for other racial and socioeconomic factors. Among the included control variables were block-group-level race, income, population density, and transit utilization. Specifically, the ACS records included the block-group percentage nonwhite, median household income, population density (log transformed), and the proportion of workers over the age of sixteen who use public transit to commute to work. As in the analyses reported in Chapter 4, these variables were intended to capture both self-interest explanations for referendum support and, more indirectly, the role of racial attitudes in support for transit.[22] For each metropolitan referendum, I estimated three nested regression models predicting transit referendum support as a function of partisanship and other Census variables.

Results from these regression models appear in Table 5.1. While the results do not conclusively test whether partisan identification has a causal effect on support for transit, they reveal that a precinct's two-party presidential vote is highly predictive of how it will vote on regional transit measures. Whether in the politically balanced but polarized Detroit area or the more Democratic and less polarized Bay Area, the relationship between partisanship and transit referendum support was very strong, holding even after alternative explanations for transit referendum support are accounted for.

In the Detroit metropolitan area, a one-standard-deviation (19-point) increase in the Democratic presidential two-party vote coincided with about an 8-point increase in precinct support for the RTA referendum, regardless of model specification. Other factors also came into play, but are usually of little explanatory importance beyond partisanship. For example, a 3-point (one-standard-deviation) increase in the proportion of a precinct's workers taking transit to work results in only a one-point increase in support for the transit referendum. For every standard deviation (19-point) difference in the nonwhite population share in a precinct, there was only a 0.8 percent increase in support for transit. Such results do not suggest that race or transit utilization are unimportant, but that they provide

Table 5.1. *Least squares regression results from the Detroit RTA referendum and San Francisco BART referendum showing the persistent relationship between partisanship and support for transit funding. Source: Center for Transportation Excellence database, county precinct-level voting returns, and American Community Survey data (Fitch and Ruggles, 2003).*

	Detroit RTA			SF BART		
	Model 1	Model 2	Model 3	Model 1	Model 2	Model 3
(Intercept)	0.245*	−0.141*	−0.203*	0.078*	0.538*	0.537*
	(0.005)	(0.057)	(0.058)	(0.006)	(0.032)	(0.032)
D two-party vote	0.425*	0.405*	0.398*	0.795*	0.784*	0.780*
	(0.007)	(0.008)	(0.009)	(0.008)	(0.010)	(0.011)
Log pop./sq km		0.027*	0.026*		−0.002	−0.002
		(0.002)	(0.002)		(0.001)	(0.001)
Log (med. income)		0.019*	0.025*		−0.037*	−0.037*
		(0.005)	(0.005)		(0.003)	(0.003)
Prop. nonwhite		0.042*	0.040*		−0.038*	−0.038*
		(0.012)	(0.012)		(0.005)	(0.005)
Prop. Hispanic		0.040	0.083*		0.001	0.003
		(0.024)	(0.026)		(0.007)	(0.008)
Prop. transit users			0.289*			0.011
			(0.069)			(0.011)
N	1,979	1,970	1,969	2,462	2,403	2,403

Notes: Standard errors in parentheses
* indicates significance at $p < 0.05$.

little explanatory power beyond what is already explained by partisan affiliation.

In the San Francisco Bay Area, which largely has less pronounced black–white racial conflict than Detroit, and where the transit system being funded is used and favored among affluent commuters in the East Bay, partisanship was even more clearly tied to transit referendum voting. For every one-standard-deviation (14-point) increase in the Clinton vote, a precinct was 11 points more likely to support the BART referendum. Surprisingly, after accounting for other factors, including the precinct-level Clinton vote, more nonwhite precincts in the Bay Area were slightly *less* likely to support the referendum, and, in contrast to Detroit, the proportion of transit commuters in a precinct had no additional bearing on referendum support. In both metropolitan areas, the large and stable coefficients on partisanship across model specifications suggest that when voters are asked to support taxes or borrowing for urban transit programs, their views are consistently aligned with their party.

This finding is consistent with many others revealing the importance of partisanship in the development of policy attitudes on complex issues (e.g., Lenz, 2009; Sniderman and Stiglitz, 2012). It also shows how much partisanship can matter to the policies adopted in metropolitan areas in seemingly nonpartisan local policy matters. More Democratic metropolitan areas are more likely to vote for measures supporting more investment in transportation, but geographic polarization can be especially important when decisions are made among jurisdictions, such as when individual municipalities and counties have voted on whether to join (or, in rare instances, secede from) regional transit authorities.[23]

Conclusion

This chapter has discussed the circumstances under which partisan geography is likely to shape transportation policy. For a number of reasons, we might expect transportation policy to be insulated from partisan polarization. Transportation politics sometimes seems to be a "policy-free zone" in Congress (Panagopoulos and Schank, 2007), marked more by distributive politics and horse trading than ideologically motivated policy making. And, at least in Congress, there is little evidence to challenge this basic intuition. Even though members of Congress have long adopted divergent preferences toward highways and their alternatives, recent polarization has not (yet) resulted in major changes in transportation policy. Notably, even as Congress has become more ideologically polarized, thus seemingly making ideology more likely to influence the transportation policy agenda (as it appeared to do in the 1960s and 1970s), partisan geographic sorting appears to have had little role in producing new or more polarizing legislation around transportation policy issues. In addition, at least as of the time of this writing, congressional institutions and the Highway Trust Fund – which ensures a steady (if insufficient) flow of revenue to transportation programs – seem to have insulated federal transportation policy making from the consequences of member polarization or the geographic polarization within metropolitan areas.

Polarized metropolitan geography is much more likely to matter in metropolitan areas, where it influences the decisions over creation and funding of regional transportation programs. This chapter has presented contemporary cross-sectional evidence illustrating how polarized metropolitan geography operates through local institutions to reduce mobility provision in metropolitan areas. Transportation policy is not a salient issue for most Americans, who mostly agree on the highways' benefits even as they disagree over alternatives to highways. To the extent that policy differences exist, partisanship appears to play a strong role, but geography and institutions interact to determine how these preferences translate into policy. Federal policy has given state and local and governments – which have long had primary responsibility over transportation improvements – more power over transportation planning and finance, placing important decisions at the mercy of local preferences. MPOs, thought to be a solution to the problem of efficient and equitable metropolitan transportation planning, adopt decisions that reflect the preferences of those who sit on MPO boards. These board members are often elected officials responsive to their own voters' preferences (Gerber and Gibson, 2009; Carney, Gerber, and Miller, 2017).

Finally, entrusting voters with direct approval over transportation finance leaves important decisions about urban-area mobility at the mercy of suburban voters' preferences. When voters have a direct voice over transportation project funding, as they do in the case of transportation funding, their votes are highly correlated with partisanship. This is especially critical for the future of central cities, which rarely have sufficient voting power on their own and rely on support from suburbanites willing to invest in urban transportation. These liberal, pro-transit suburban allies are much more likely to appear in more Democratic suburbs. Their absence in more conservative and Republican suburbs can forestall regional transportation solutions entirely. The evidence here shows that strong anti-urban biases and ideological disagreements that are now increasingly tied to partisanship may be difficult to overcome.

Notes

1 These search terms included the words "road," "highway," "bus," "'rail," "train," and "transit." To further code bills related to highways and transit, a hierarchical coding scheme was adopted to isolate particular types of legislation.

2 Each bill was coded by two research assistants (RAs) who coded a subset of three hundred bills, then discussed their rules for coding and disagreements. They continued this process, coding large blocks of bills mostly independently, while discussing possible disagreements or coding ambiguities.

3 If a bill was coded as delivering program funding to a specific state or local set of states (for example, for a river bridge between two states), the bill was coded as particularistic and the benefiting states were recorded.

4 "Urban" and "nonurban" are coded according to a binary variable provided in Adler (2014): whether, according to the Statistical Abstract, "a district contains or is contained in one of the fifty largest central cities" (Adler, 2014; Codebook, 3).

5 The subsuming of highways and transit under a massive formula-based funding bill could also be read as an example of "institutionalization" in Congress, with individual members now have less latitude to introduce vanity legislation around transportation topics (Polsby, 1968).

6 A few bills to limit federal transit programs appear in the data. These were not coded under the described scheme.

7 See especially Patashnik (1997, 441).

8 The adverse consequences of devolution in social welfare policy offer useful parallels to the transportation case. See Soss, Fording, and Schram (2008); Michener (2018).

9 Moynihan wrote an influential and prescient critical essay about the urban highway program shortly after the start of the program (Moynihan, 1960).

10 For the history of the politics around the ISTEA MPO provisions and their early implementation, see Weingroff (2001); Rose and Mohl (2012).

11 As of 2006, eleven MPOs provided some (unspecified) compensatory votes to more populous municipalities, and another five allow for population-weighted voting rules invoked on an ad hoc basis by board members (Sanchez, 2006, 13).

12 Several aspects of MPO organization may partially mitigate representational biases. State transportation department representatives often sit on the boards and exercise substantial behind-the-scenes influence over projects (Gerber and Gibson, 2009). MPO boards tend to defer to the judgment of permanent staff and vote by unanimous consent, which may counter cities' disadvantages under formal voting rules. As Sanchez (2006) notes, "Following the practices of many COGs [councils of government], split votes are avoided whenever possible. The boards delay addressing controversial issues and avoid weighted voting to maintain an ostensibly collaborative atmosphere among members" (5). Such consensus-based decision-making can help urban and pro-urban governments as they seek concessions from the suburban voting majority, but still leaves them relatively weakened.

13 The correlation of the dissimilarity index and suburban overrepresentation on MPOs is 0.09, and 0.18 when the correlation is weighted by MPO population.

14 One of the most cited works on this topic, Nelson et al. (2004), observes that "expenditure information by type of transportation investment is simply not tracked over time by most MPOs in a way that can be accessed remotely. Even when asked, most MPOs could not generate such information" (7).

15 In regressions using the Sanchez measures of urban voting power, combined with data from Gerber and Gibson (2009), I find no evidence that greater urban voting power contributes to differences in support for local versus regional projects. However, it may matter to the urban–suburban distribution of projects. Gerber and Gibson (2009) report particularistic versus general transportation projects, but do not report the urban–suburban distribution.

16 Unlike the other studies cited here, An and Bostic (2017) is based on projects actually funded, not just those planned or approved by the MPO.

17 For an account of the politics of these taxes, see Wachs (2003); Crabbe et al. (2005); Green (2014).

18 In the most notorious example of county voting on regional transportation programs, the Metropolitan Atlanta Rapid Transit Agency

was voted down by multiple counties whose support was crucial to the development of the system. Cobb County voted against participating in a regional system in 1965, and Gwinnett and Clayton counties declined to increase sales taxes to join the MARTA system in 1971 (Schroeder and Sjoquist, 1978; Bayor, 1996; Monroe, 2012; Wickert, 2016). These local votes have been widely seen as examples of (predominantly white) suburban resistance to transit investment, but they can also be understood as bellwethers of conservative suburban resistance to transit expansion.

19 The four counties included in the RTA were Macomb, Oakland, Wayne, and Washtenaw.

20 In addition to the demographic and political differences between the Detroit and San Francisco areas, transit operates quite differently in the two regions. For example, in the Detroit area, only thirty-one voting precincts (1.5 percent of precincts) have transit-commuting rates over 10 percent, versus 1,497 precincts (60 percent) in the BART service area.

21 In California, precinct shapefiles were obtained from Schleuss, Fox, and Krishnakumar (2017).

22 Because full Census data are not recorded at the precinct level, I joined the data sources together by converting the precinct shapefile and ACS block-group polygon shapefiles into points, then performed a nearest-neighbor point-to-point spatial join in ArcGIS.

23 Such regional noncooperation also takes forms other than funding votes. Votes to secede from transportation authorities or districts, or to block local support for extensions of regional transportation projects such as light rail, uniformly originate in suburban, rural, and more Republican areas. Early votes on Atlanta's MARTA were only one example, but others have appeared in recent years. In Tigard, Oregon, for example, local opposition to construction of the Southwest extension of Portland's MAX light rail service precipitated a change to the city charter that required voters to approve any involvement in the light rail system, and a mandated referendum passed by only a narrow margin. In Perrysburg, Sylvania Township, and Spencer Township, Ohio, predominantly rural suburban and Republican voters (who had both pocketbook and ideological reasons not to support a predominantly urban transit system) held votes in 2012 to withdraw from the Toledo Area Regional Transportation Authority (TARTA) (Patch, 2012). Supporters of such secession referenda typically argue that transit agencies are poorly managed (often, a well-founded accusation) and that suburban and rural residents do not use the services.

6 | Conclusion

Spatial policies from highways and transit to housing and community development influence who lives where, with long-lasting implications for the political geography of the country's metropolitan areas. One of the most important spatial policies has been the creation of new infrastructure facilitating suburbanization, facilitating a larger urban–suburban partisan divide over the postwar period. This *partisan geographic polarization* was facilitated, in no small part, by the construction of federally subsidized highways, and especially the Interstate Highway System, across the postwar era. The federal highway program provided states the funding needed to build highways that have helped expand their suburban areas (Baum-Snow, 2007a), thus enabling the migration of white, middle- and upper-income, and other Republican-leaning groups into suburban communities. The geography of partisanship and issue politics have changed in the process.

Democrats and Republicans have had different residential preferences since at least the 1970s, but their means to act on them were limited until the building of modern highways. Real-world limitations have forced partisans not to act on their residential preferences, as other priorities take precedence over finding socially or politically "compatible" communities (Hui, 2013). For example, Americans strongly prefer to live near their jobs in affordable, quality neighborhoods, with the partisan and social makeup of those neighborhoods usually considered only secondarily (Mummolo and Nall, 2017). Federally funded highways enabled Americans to choose from a wider range of housing and employment options, and, in the process, allowed them to move to communities more compatible with their secondary preferences with no net loss in personal utility. Highway-induced residential migration has created more polarized metropolitan areas in the process.

The resulting partisan geographic divide, coinciding with suburban-ization and white flight, would seem likely to be marked by policy attitudes driven by urban and suburban residents' household-level material concerns. This intuition has been central to scholarship on the politics of suburbanization: that citizens of urban, suburban, and rural areas adopt different policy perspectives because they live in different places with different material policy demands. The logic of "policy feedback (Pierson, 1993; Soss, 2000; Mettler, 2002; Campbell, 2003) suggests that those who settled in the suburbs, depending on automobiles and suburban transportation infrastructure, would become more supportive of additional highway spending. By this logic, those who remained in cities, relying to a greater extent on urban transportation systems, would become stronger supporters of mass transit and related transportation investments. Transportation policy appears to be the epitome of place-based policy likely to elicit parochial, localized interests.

What I have found in public opinion, institutions, and voting data instead suggests a more complex explanation than a simple account of suburbanites as a special interest. Rather than directly reflecting direct economic or place-based interests, transportation policies either elicit broad bipartisan agreement or yield ideological disagreements over redistributive aspects of transportation policy. However, attitudes on transportation policy cannot be neatly described as "urban" or "suburban." Highways attract broad, bipartisan support that does not vary substantially as a function of the population density of Americans' places of residence, suggesting that the stereotypical por-trayal of American highway supporters as white, suburban, and conservative is generally misplaced. When Americans are asked to consider funding of competing transportation policies as a zero-sum game, disagreement over transportation policy grows substantially and is more clearly associated with partisanship. The more a trans-portation policy entails services that aid the poor or urban residents, the more substantially Democrats and Republicans disagree over the policy, regardless of their place of residence. In short, it appears that liberal and conservative ideologies are substantially intruding into transportation politics in ways that overwhelm interest-based explanations.

When Americans are asked questions about transportation policy, their answers suggest that their self-interest as transportation users has minimal effect beyond what is already tied up in their partisan identity. The density of one's place of residence generally has very little to do with transportation policy attitudes beyond what can be explained by partisanship. Personal factors such as residential population density, race, and income do appear to matter more when people are forced to make choices between competing transportation priorities (Chapter 4). However, even under these circumstances, partisanship does more to explain differences on a host of controversial policies.

The lack of evidence of a "place-based interest" beyond what is captured by partisanship suggests three equally plausible explanations. First, as more Republicans have resided in the suburbs, the party's policy concerns have shifted away from solving urban problems, as evidenced in the Republican platform (Baker, 2012). As the national party becomes more supportive of nonurban interests generally and more opposed to urban investments such as transit and public housing, Republican voters may respond more to this cue than to their own experience. Second, population density might not matter to public opinion to any great extent because the variation in population density over which most Americans live is, in fact, insufficient to affect policy attitudes on subjects such as highways and transit, since so few Americans used transportation modes other than personal vehicles. As Pisarski (2006) documents, high nonautomobile commuting rates are to be found only in New York City and the most densely populated zip codes of a few other metropolitan areas. Elsewhere, commuters of all political stripes typically use their personal automobiles in their travel to work. So, the difference in population density between a *typical* urban and rural American may be inconsequential, suggesting that we cannot completely reject place-based interests as an explanation. In their place, partisanship and ideology appear to be shaping policy attitudes and prompting Americans to support policies (such as urban transit systems) in which they have at most an indirect material interest. Third, transportation policy attitudes may not be associated with features of one's place of residence for the same reason that Americans support other policies from which they do not directly benefit. They may perceive an indirect benefit (such as traffic reduction or environmental benefits), or their support may reflect ideological or motivated reasoning. For example, just as partisans change policy evaluations due to messages from party elites, they may adopt the "correct" position around transportation and other urban policies.

Democrats may believe that transit is more environmentally friendly (e.g., reducing greenhouse gas emissions and taking cars off the road) because that message has been conveyed by party elites.

Whatever its origins, the link between partisanship and ideology explains why urban–suburban *geographic* polarization is important to policy. While many reasons exist to care about the consequences of geographic polarization, this book shows that polarization matters not just because of its effects on legislative politics, but also because of its effects on more local institutions and public goods provision (Orfield, 1994; Gerber and Gibson, 2009). Metropolitan geographic polarization matters not only because it might isolate the flow of diverse political information (though the evidence for this is sparse) (Gentzkow and Shapiro, 2011) or because of polarization of state legislatures or congressional delegations, but because polarized attitudes may undermine support for the provision of specific types of public goods. Among the most important of these are the transportation investments that facilitate Americans' mobility.

Why Is Partisanship, Not Race, Central to This Account?

One possible reaction to the findings presented throughout this book is that they are far too focused on partisanship, when, in fact, it could be argued that race and racial attitudes are the prime mover of many of the partisan and geographic changes observed here. One measure of geographic polarization, the metropolitan level precinct dissimilarity index (Massey and Denton, 1988), is correlated with a metropolitan area's black population proportion at $r = 0.84$, a value so high that if applied to survey items it would suggest that the two items are measuring the same basic concept.[1] However, partisanship has become a more salient social identity in its own right, and focusing entirely on race as the prime explanation for observed politics would fail to account for ways that race has not been the sole cleavage driving changes in partisan identification or partisan geographic polarization (Iyengar, Sood, and Lelkes, 2012; Iyengar and Westwood, 2015). Nor is partisan geographic polarization interchangeable with racial polarization. The metropolitan-level dissimilarity indexes for precinct-level black composition and partisan composition are correlated at $r = .42$, which confirms a strong relationship between racial and partisan segregation, while still indicating that partisan and racial segregation are far from collinear. Even after accounting for the race of individual survey respondents or the racial composition of voting precincts in statistical models, partisanship remains a major cleavage delineating local transportation policy attitudes. My approach throughout this book has been to acknowledge the role of race in the development of the contemporary party system and metropolitan politics without treating partisan geographic polarization as a second-order effect or epiphenomenon of metropolitan racial composition.

Even if racial sorting and white flight were a more appropriate focus of the sorting analysis, the results in this book indicate the important *partisan* mechanism by which diversity might lead to worse public goods provision.[2] Local partisans may receive issue messages from national, state, and local partisan elites. Attitudes toward transportation policy, a generally low-salience issue area, may be shaped by these partisan messages. And, tellingly, in recent years, Republican politicians have campaigned in favor of investments in highways while proposing disinvestment in other transportation alternatives, and such messages (sometimes conveyed via conservative media such as talk radio) may very well be contributing to voters' growing partisan differences over transportation policy. For example, in 2010, Wisconsin State Rep. Scott Walker, then a candidate for governor, lamented that a heavily used suburban interchange had not been fixed because of "Milwaukee politicians fighting work on the East–West corridor," the Interstate highway (I-94) running through Milwaukee's heavily Republican suburbs (Held, 2010).

Similar messages have been sent by conservative Republicans in Congress, who in recent years have proposed – but have rarely succeeded in passing – bills and amendments to fund highways while zeroing out mass transit funding. For example, in 2011, the Republican Study Committee proposed eliminating subsidies to Amtrak, the Washington Metro, and the New Starts transit program, which pays for new transit systems (Jordan, 2011). These programs have remained on the books even as Republicans have attempted to challenge them and as the two parties have traded control of Congress and the presidency in recent decades (Freemark, 2011). At the state level, Republicans have been more successful at halting high-speed rail projects and other nonhighway transportation programs, signaling to their constituents that such programs are wasteful projects serving urban and Democratic constituencies.

Assessing the Broader Implications of Geographic Polarization

Of course, if partisan geographic polarization matters – and I show that it likely does matter to public policy – it has many consequences beyond the ones outlined in this book. While this book has focused almost entirely on geographic polarization's implications for transportation policy, Democrats and Republicans' geographic distribution matters for reasons beyond transportation policy outcomes. One of the most widely mentioned consequences mentioned by pundits, but rarely supported by evidence, is the "echo chamber" effect: that polarization matters because partisan geographic sorting deprives Americans of access to alternative political viewpoints. Other discussions of polarized geography are more attentive to the wide array of electoral and distributive outcomes that derive directly from partisan geography. How polarized geography affects urban transportation policy is clearly a case of the latter, but there is a multitude of policy implications.

In this book, I have deliberately avoided whether partisan geographic polarization has contextual (neighborhood) effects on political behavior or in the creation of informational "echo chambers." This concern, articulated in *The Big Sort* (Bishop and Cushing, 2008) and repeated by political pundits, motivates much of the research on polarization. In fact, the initial impetus for this book arose in part from my reading of Bill Bishop's page-turner about American polarization in summer 2008. Unfortunately, such work is often marked by hyperbole about polarization present in American social life. Schier and Eberly (2016), for instance, write that "geographic echo chambers" of sorted communities result in people having "little opportunity to engage with people who may have a different perspective." In a recent online piece, *The Cook Political Report*'s US House editor David Wasserman discussed the "disappearance of purple America," as more people live in landslide counties, introducing the risk that "an entire generation of Americans will grow up without exposure to alternative points of view" (Wasserman, 2017). One very well could imagine scenarios under which political isolation limits exposure to alternative viewpoints, especially for those living in completely homogeneous partisan areas.

Such isolated communities are exceedingly rare, and it is important to distinguish the results that I present in this book from such strong claims about partisans' alleged social isolation. Few American communities are so homogeneous that Americans will be completely isolated from alternative viewpoints, even if they were somehow dependent on their neighbors for political ideas and information. For example, if we classify a zip code in which one party won 80 percent of the two-party presidential vote in 2008 as an "isolated" information environment, only 10 percent of zip codes meet this threshold (about half of these isolated environments are Democratic, half Republican). These homogeneous zip codes are often in areas dominated by an ethnic, a racial, or a religious group with a longstanding history of partisan bloc voting. For example, about one-third of zip codes in the states of Wyoming, Louisiana, and Utah were this homogeneous (and almost all Republican), while about a quarter of zip codes in Hawaii and New Mexico were over 80 percent Democratic. Elsewhere, segregated black neighborhoods also have few Republican voters.

Even if there were a basis for concern about the social isolation of partisans, the idea that creating more diverse local political environments would necessarily result in more heterogeneous political interactions is unsupported. The available evidence suggests that exposure to political disagreement, far from leading people to entertain and absorb opposing viewpoints, can actually have the opposite effect: causing political "deviants" to "hunker down" (Putnam, 2007), sometimes with like-minded people (Finifter, 1974) and to withdraw from participation. This can reduce participation and engagement by members of the political minority (Mutz, 2002). Localized political diversity may result in different interactions, but this does not mean that Americans will accept political views from neighbors with whom they disagree. The available evidence suggests that Americans are not turning to their immediate neighbors for discussion and information in the first place. For example, Americans report that they rarely talk to their neighbors, and when they do, their conversations rarely turn to politics (Abrams and Fiorina, 2012).[3] In fact, a consequence of localized (nonpolitical) diversity, which can coincide with political diversity, may be to limit the number of such interactions and reduce local engagement (Putnam, 2007). Partisan sorting within one's primary group – such as in the selection of one's spouse or domestic partner – is potentially more consequential to exchange of political information and socialization, but this type of sorting is only indirectly affected by partisan geography (Iyengar, Sood, and Lelkes, 2012; Hersh and Ghitza, 2017).

Attempting to nail down psychological and contextual effects of partisan segregation and focusing on geographic "echo chambers" may distract from more important implications of geographic polarization: that polarized partisan geography will dictate who gets elected, and how responsive representatives seek to deliver benefits to their constituents. In short, partisan geography partially dictates "who gets what, why, and how," in Harold Lasswell's oft-quoted words. This book has considered how and where partisan geographic polarization determines the answer to these questions. I have shown that partisan geography and metropolitan polarization can matter greatly to the politics of mobility in metropolitan areas. However, similar consequences are likely to appear in other policy domains as well: in regional infrastructure (water, sewer, and electricity), education (K–12 and community college districts), housing programs, and health and welfare programs (such as public hospitals). Central cities now rarely account for the majority of the population in a metropolitan area and are reliant on their economically prosperous suburbs. Urban–suburban polarization is therefore likely to dictate whether central cities are able to win needed support for needed programs.

Moreover, urban–suburban polarization is likely to have its greatest impact when voters in a metropolitan area are asked to invest in regional programs with redistributive implications. Regional political geography will likely impact multiple correlated policy domains connected by partisanship. For example, in the 2016 Bay Area Rapid Transit bond referendum discussed in Chapter 5, the Alameda County precinct-level two-party Democratic presidential vote was correlated with the bond referendum at 0.62. For Measure A1, the county's successful $580 million affordable housing bond referendum, the precinct-level presidential and referendum vote shares were correlated at $r = 0.81$.[4]

The Politics of Spatial Policy and the Future of American Opportunity

Spatial policies such as highways remake physical geography, thereby changing social and political geography. While the geographic distribution of voters is of little consequence on its own, it does matter anywhere there is geographic representation, in settings as obvious as municipal governments, state legislatures, and Congress, and in more obscure bodies such as MPOs or special district boards. When partisans are ideologically consistent, geographic polarization may well become a harbinger of geographically rooted, ideologically driven disputes. The consequences are likely to be especially pronounced for spatial policies themselves: geographic polarization will affect implementation of programs that are distributed on the basis of place.

Policy-induced geographic polarization interacts with institutions to determine how policies are implemented. In the context of the American highway system, one of the most important of these factors is delivery of federal matching funds combined with devolution of planning authority to states and local governments. A well-known risk of such devolution is that policy federalism induces states to rely on federal funding and make poor fiscal decisions (Peterson, 1995; Rodden, 2006). It also transfers the scope of political conflict over implementation to lower geographic units, subjecting federally financed policies to the whims of state and local governments and program administrators (Mettler, 1998). With partisans adopting differing attitudes toward urban areas and over investment in urban policy, responsive state and local planning bodies responsible for policy implementation are likely to adopt decisions that reflect the configuration of partisans. As a result, formation of city–suburban coalitions (Orfield, 1994; Weir, Wolman, and Swanstrom, 2005), which have been shown to be critical to the expansion of metropolitan programs, will be impeded not just because of differing "place-based" interests, but because of polarized partisan geography. This will almost surely result in biases in program administration, as Chapter 5 demonstrates. The federal-aid highway program therefore has much in common with other federal matching programs, including Medicaid, which allows state and local administrators considerable discretion in program administration, often to the detriment of the poor and politically underrepresented (Mashaw, 1971; Soss, 2000; Michener, 2018).

This work has also illuminated partisan politics' role in creating the "geography of opportunity" in metropolitan areas (Chetty et al., 2014). While there has been much recent speculation about why the poor in some areas have better *economic* mobility and life outcomes, the findings in this book suggest that federal transportation programs as implemented at the local level may provide an explanation. Chetty et al. (2014) found that the correlation between sprawl (commuting time) and their measure of upward income mobility is .61 (6). In no small part, these differences are sustained by urban–suburban polarization and affluent suburbanites' disproportionate influence over metropolitan transportation policy, which determines metropolitan investments in transportation programs. While more research is needed, this political model is a possible explanation of the persistent link between sprawl and economic opportunity.

This book therefore suggests a new direction for research on urban political economy, which has, up to this point, varied between two extremes. At one extreme are theoretical models of the political economy of development backed by qualitative case studies, process tracing, and thick description of urban coalitional politics. From regime theory (Stone, 1989) to growth machines (Logan and Molotch, 2007), this scholarship has harkened back to the community power debate and questions about the nature of city power (Bachrach and Baratz, 1963; Merelman, 1968; Dahl, 2005). At the other extreme, economists have tended to focus on the specific effects of policy interventions on urban form and on labor and housing markets (e.g., Anas, Arnott, and Small, 1998; Glaeser and Kahn, 2004; Glaeser, Gyourko, and Saks, 2006). Glaeser and Kahn (2004), for example, use national gasoline tax levels as an instrument for car ownership to estimate highways' effects on population density and sprawl (2503). This work, focused as it is on the interaction of policies and metropolitan real estate and labor markets, often focuses on ways that government policy is a distorting force in local markets. A political science approach rooted in solid empirical approaches can make urban *politics* and metropolitan political institutions more central to urban political economy research (Trounstine, 2009, 2015).

My research also suggests the need for American politics researchers to incorporate spatial policies, their political consequences, and their long-term effects on various forms of inequality. To be sure, there has already been much work on the role of "laws of the landscape" (Nivola, 1999), explaining how the United States is exceptional, among Organization for Economic Cooperation and Development (OECD) countries, in its per capita energy consumption and policies favoring the automobile. In the United States, there has been extensive research on de jure racial segregation (Massey and Denton, 1993), government-supported redlining by banks and insurance companies (Jackson, 1980; Hillier, 2003; Glock, 2016), and exclusionary residential zoning (Levine, 2006; Hirt, 2014). While such exclusionary policies have been analyzed at length, and their impacts seem to be well known, the changing political regime that sustains them often receives less attention. Similarly, economic and environmental historians have examined the economic impacts of railroads (Fogel, 1964; White, 2011; Donaldson, 2016; Donaldson and Hornbeck, 2016), highways (Baum-Snow, 2007*a*), and water distribution projects (Reisner, 1993), among other infrastructure projects. In examining economic or environmental impacts, these accounts can neglect the role partisan politics plays in sustaining these policies.[5] This is critical because, in many cases, such developmental spatial policies have facilitated the localized growth of one of the two major parties.[6]

Study of spatial policies is doubly important as the United States continues to debate the meaning and gravity of its infrastructure crisis. At the time of this writing, the Federal Transit Administration had just placed the Washington Metro under emergency orders for serious electrical problems that threatened to shut down large sections of the system for repairs. Flint, Michigan, had recently emerged from a public health crisis arising from the corrosion of the city's lead water service pipes after the city shifted its water supply to a less expensive source. In each case, local and state governments (including special-purpose governments) had made decisions that compromised the health and safety of service users. In the case of Flint, Michigan, the resulting problems produced a volley of partisan accusations. Regardless of the institutional responsibility (and there is much to go around), any sincere effort to fix "crumbling" infrastructure of all kinds will require devoting more resources to cities with aging infrastructure stock. If past is prologue, we can expect the battle lines on these issues to be drawn along partisan lines.

In the face of these local challenges now tied up in polarized politics, the temptation facing some urban advocates has been to avoid or circumvent politics altogether. Just as they did in the last century, transportation modernizers are discussing solving the problems of urban transportation with technology. But as new technology – from "smart cities" to autonomous vehicles – offers to revolutionize transportation, housing, and the uses of urban space, the themes that I address in this work will remain important as ever. Transportation policy makers and present-day urban boosters seem poised to accept privately developed technological solutions to what are, fundamentally, political struggles over the distribution of resources. These political struggles, playing out over time and along urban–suburban lines, have yielded an urban transportation system dedicated to the single-occupancy vehicle. Technological innovation, including the development of autonomous vehicles, holds the allure of improving on or even overturning this longstanding spatial regime, perhaps even blurring the lines between existing transportation alternatives such as transit and private automobiles. (Self-driving automobiles need not be stored in a location within walking distance of their passengers, thus freeing them to be used by multiple riders.) Optimists expect self-driving cars eventually to overcome the limitations of the modern automobile.

Just as the expansion of mass automobility required public investments in transportation infrastructure to make the technology useful, so new transportation technologies will require new supporting public infrastructure. These new needs are likely to bring up the same challenging issues around federalism and the geographic distribution of transportation benefits. As these new technologies develop, the risk is that engineers and technical planners will be entrusted with adapting cities to the new technology by "technical" and "rational" means, just as they did in the 1940s and 1950s, without considering how decisions over public infrastructure are political and involve the selection of winners and losers. State highway departments staffed by "production-oriented" engineers once understood their task as developing the most efficient means of conducting traffic along "desire lines" of greatest existing demand (Mickle, 1952), but public opposition robbed them of this discretion (though not before the Interstate program was substantially complete; Rose and Seely (1990).[7] A new generation of autonomous vehicle and "smart city" engineers may find themselves thrust into the same role.

The logic of high modernism (Scott, 1998) provided a rationale for massive highway projects and urban renewal. Those involved either did not realize or did not deeply consider how the programs would undermine metropolitan areas and empower suburbs. Attempts to remedy these shortcomings have come up against the political realities of a federal transportation program and local transportation policy discretion. The problems outlined in this book are unlikely to disappear merely because of transportation modernization – and, if anything, are likely to become even more salient. In the words of architectural critic Lewis Mumford, speaking at a 1957 conference on the new Interstate Highway System, "As Clemenceau said of war, it is too important to be left to the experts and the specialists [sic], so I suppose one should say of highway planning." These words are prophetic as ever as technology and engineering proficiency are again being offered as a panacea for urban mobility challenges in a polarized nation. Transportation infrastructure creates opportunity, but, as we have seen, it can also become a catalyst for sorting, polarization, and spatial stratification.

Notes

1 Removing high-leverage outliers (for example, the New Orleans metropolitan area) only slightly reduces this relationship.
2 For related findings on race and political geography, see Hersh and Nall (2016).
3 Even when Americans select the type of political information and news they would like to consume (a much lower-cost and lower-stakes decision than residential choice), people are often omnivorous in the ideological selection of media and online political information (Gentzkow and Shapiro, 2011; Mummolo, 2016).
4 A nonrandom sample of precinct-level votes in other transit and transportation tax referenda and conducted in recent years in California, Florida, and Georgia revealed similarly high correlations between the two-party presidential vote and support for transportation taxes (Center for Transportation Excellence, 2017).
5 However, for recent work on the politics of railroad construction, see Callen (2016).
6 In the Mountain West, for example, the rapid growth of a predominantly Republican region in the twentieth century can be traced back to the federal Bureau of Reclamation's massive dam projects, ostensibly intended to support agriculture, but ultimately critical to the region's urban growth. Notably, the Western states that have benefited most from dam projects (and would be sparsely populated but for federal projects) were or eventually became Republican bastions (Stewart and Weingast, 1992).
7 For classic work on the development of technical expertise in urban policy making and reform, see Wiebe (1966).

Bibliography

Abrams, Samuel and Morris Fiorina. 2012. "'The Big Sort That Wasn't': A Skeptical Reexamination." *PS: Political Science and Politics* 45(2): 203–10.

Adler, E. Scott. 2014. "Congressional District Data 80th–113th Congress." Accessed August 1, 2015. URL: *http://bit.ly/2hq6Lhc*

Adler, E. Scott and John D. Wilkerson. 2014. *Congress and the Politics of Problem Solving.* Cambridge, UK: Cambridge University Press.

Adler, E. Scott and John Wilkerson. 2015. "Congressional Bills Project, 1947–2014." Accessed January 1, 2015. URL: *www.congressionalbills .org*

Agrawal, Asha Weinstein, and Hilary Nixon. 2011*a*. "What Do Americans Think About Federal Transportation Tax Options? Results from a National Survey." Technical Report 10-12 Mineta Transportation Institute, San José State University, San Jose, CA. Accessed July 22, 2015. URL: *http://transweb.sjsu.edu/project/1031.html*

2011*b*. "What Do Americans Think About Federal Transportation Tax Options? Results from Year 2 of a National Survey." Technical Report 10-12 Mineta Transportation Institute, San José State University, San Jose, CA. Accessed July 22, 2015. URL: *http://transweb.sjsu.edu/ project/1031.html*

2013. "What Do Americans Think About Federal Tax Options to Support Public Transit, Highways, and Local Streets and Roads? Results from Year Four of a National Survey." Technical Report 12-07 Mineta Transportation Institute, San José State University, San Jose, CA. Accessed July 22, 2015. URL: *http://transweb.sjsu.edu/project/ 1228.html*

2014. "What Do Americans Think About Federal Tax Options to Support Public Transit, Highways, and Local Streets and Roads? Results from Year Five of a National Survey." Technical Report 12-36 Mineta Transportation Institute, San José State University, San Jose, CA. Accessed July 22, 2015. URL: *http://transweb.sjsu.edu/project/ 1328.html*

148

2015. "What Do Americans Think About Federal Tax Options to Support Public Transit, Highways, and Local Streets and Roads? Results from Year Six of a National Survey." Technical Report 12-51 Mineta Transportation Institute, San José State University, San Jose, CA. Accessed July 22, 2015. URL: *http://transweb.sjsu.edu/project/1428.html*

Agrawal, Asha Weinstein, Hilary Nixon, and Clayton Nall. 2017. "No Democratic Roads or Republican Roads? Partisanship and the Making of Transportation Policy Attitudes." In *Compendium of Papers, Transportation Research Board Annual Meeting*. Washington, DC. Accessed January 8, 2017. URL: *http://bit.ly/2ph7Gyo*

Agrawal, Asha Weinstein, Hilary Nixon, and Vinay Murthy. 2012. "What Do Americans Think About Federal Tax Options to Support Public Transit, Highways, and Local Streets and Roads? Results from Year Three of a National Survey." Technical Report 12-01 Mineta Transportation Institute, San José State University, San Jose, CA. Accessed July 22, 2015. URL: *http://transweb.sjsu.edu/project/1228.html*

Alonso, William. 1964. *Location and Land Use*. Cambridge, MA: Harvard University Press.

Altshuler, Alan and David Luberoff. 2003. *Mega-Projects: The Changing Politics of Urban Public Investment*. Washington, DC: Brookings Institution Press and Lincoln Institute of Land Policy.

American Political Science Association. Task Force on Inequality and American Democracy. 2004. "American Democracy in an Age of Rising Inequality." Accessed May 24, 2016. URL: *http://bit.ly/2pSyAP6*

An, Brian and Raphael Bostic. 2017. "The Power of Local Governments in Regional Governance and the Distribution of Public Investment." Paper presented at the Midwest Political Science Association Annual Meeting.

Anas, Alex, Richard Arnott, and Kenneth A. Small. 1998. "Urban Spatial Structure." *Journal of Economic Literature* 36(3):1426–64.

Ansolabehere, Stephen and Eitan Hersh. 2012. "Validation: What Big Data Reveal About Survey Misreporting and the Real Electorate." *Political Analysis* 20(4):437–59.

Ansolabehere, Stephen and Jonathan Rodden. 2012. "Harvard Election Data Archive." Data file. Accessed June 1, 2012. URL: *http://projects.iq.harvard.edu/eda*

Arai, Mahmood. 2011. Cluster-Robust Standard Errors Using R. Technical Report, Stockholm University. Accessed November 10, 2017. URL: *http://bit.ly/2jgJJKe*

Atack, Jeremy. 2013. "On the Use of Geographic Information Systems in Economic History: The American Transportation Revolution Revisited." *Journal of Economic History* 73(2):313–38.

Automotive Safety Foundation. 1964. *What Freeways Mean to Your City*. Washington, DC: Automotive Safety Foundation.

Bachrach, Peter and Morton S. Baratz. 1963. "Decisions and Nondecisions: An Analytical Framework." *American Political Science Review* 57(3):632–42.

Baker, Kevin. 2012. "Republicans to Cities: Drop Dead." *New York Times* (October 6): SR1.

Balz, Daniel J. and Ronald Brownstein. 1996. *Storming the Gates: Protest Politics and the Republican Revival*. Boston: Little, Brown.

Bartels, Larry M. 2003. "Democracy with Attitudes." In *Electoral Democracy*, ed. Michael B. MacKuen and George Rabinowitz. Ann Arbor, MI: University of Michigan Press. pp. 48–82.

Baum-Snow, Nathaniel. 2007*a*. "Did Highways Cause Suburbanization?" *Quarterly Journal of Economics* 122(2):775–805.

2007*b*. "Suburbanization and Transportation in the Monocentric Model." *Journal of Urban Economics* 62(3):405–23.

Bayor, R. H. 1996. *Race and the Shaping of Twentieth-Century Atlanta*. Chapel Hill, NC: University of North Carolina Press.

Becker, Richard A., John M. Chambers, and Allan R. Wilks. 1988. *The New S Language*. New York, NY: Wadsworth.

Belden, Russonello and Stewart. 2011. *2011 National Community Preference Survey*. Washington, DC: National Association of Realtors.

Berry, Christopher. 2001. "Land Use Regulation and Residential Segregation: Does Zoning Matter?" *American Law and Economics Review* 3(2):251–74.

Bishop, Bill and Robert Cushing. 2008. *The Big Sort: Why the Clustering of Like-Minded America Is Tearing Us Apart*. Boston, MA: Houghton Mifflin.

Black, Earl and Merle Black. 2002. *The Rise of Southern Republicans*. Cambridge, MA: Harvard University Press.

Burns, Nancy. 1994. *The Formation of American Local Governments*. Oxford, UK: Oxford University Press.

Burns, Nancy, Laura Evans, Gerald Gamm, and Corrine McConnaughy. 2009. "Urban Politics in the State Arena." *Studies in American Political Development* 23(1):1–22.

Callen, Zachary. 2016. *Railroads and American Political Development: Infrastructure, Federalism, and State Building*. Lawrence, KS: University Press of Kansas.

Campbell, Andrea L. 2003. *How Policies Make Citizens: Senior Political Activism and the American Welfare State.* Princeton, NJ: Princeton University Press.

Carney, Nicholas, Elisabeth Gerber, and Susan Miller. 2017. "Choice and Design in the Designation of Metropolitan Planning Organizations." Paper presented at the Midwest Political Science Association Annual Meeting.

Center for Transportation Excellence. 2017. "Transportation Ballot Measures." Online. Accessed June 1, 2017. URL: *http://bit.ly/2tjiWkU*

Chen, Jowei and Jonathan Rodden. 2013. "Unintentional Gerrymandering: Political Geography and Electoral Bias in Legislatures." *Quarterly Journal of Political Science* 8:239–69.

Chetty, Raj, Nathaniel Hendren, Patrick Kline, and Emmanuel Saez. 2014. "Where Is the Land of Opportunity: The Geography of Intergenerational Mobility in the United States." *Quarterly Journal of Economics* 129:1553–623. Data available at www.equality-of-opportunity.org. Accessed October 1, 2017. URL: *http://bit.ly/2qElhEV*

Cho, Wendy Tam, James G. Gimpel, and Iris S. Hui. 2012. "Voter Migration and the Geographic Sorting of the American Electorate." *Annals of the Association of American Geographers* 102(2). DOI:10.1080/00045608.2012.720229.

Cohen, Lizabeth. 2004. *A Consumer's Republic: The Politics of Consumption in Postwar America.* New York, NY: Vintage.

Congressional Budget Office. 2015. "Public Spending on Transportation and Water Infrastructure, 1956 to 2014." Online. Accessed July 13, 2017. URL: *http://bit.ly/2tRFPsw*

Converse, Philip E. 1970. "Attitudes and Non-attitudes: Continuation of a Dialogue." *Quantitative Analysis of Social Problems* 168:189.

Cox, Wendell and Jean Love. 1996. The Best Investment a Nation Ever Made: A Tribute to the Dwight D. Eisenhower System of Interstate and Defense Highways. Technical Report, American Highway Users Alliance. Accessed November 10, 2017. URL: *www.publicpurpose .com/freewaypdf.pdf*

Crabbe, Amber E., Rachel Hiatt, Susan D. Poliwka, and Martin Wachs. 2005. "Local Transportation Sales Taxes: California's Experiment in Transportation Finance." *Public Budgeting & Finance* 25(3):91–121. Accessed April 2, 2017. URL: *http://bit.ly/2lVeqFs*

Dahl, Robert A. 2005. *Who Governs? Democracy and Power in an American City.* New Haven, CT: Yale University Press.

Danielson, Michael N. 1976. *The Politics of Exclusion.* New York, NY: Columbia University Press.

Dilger, Robert Jay. 2011. Federalism Issues in Surface Transportation Policy: Past and Present. Technical Report Congressional Research Service Washington, DC. Accessed July 1, 2017. URL: *http://bit.ly/2sd2gXP*

Donaldson, Dave. 2016. "Railroads of the Raj: Estimating the Impact of Transportation Infrastructure." *American Economic Review.* Forthcoming. Accessed November 10, 2017. URL: *www.nber.org/papers/w16487*

Donaldson, Dave and Richard Hornbeck. 2016. "Railroads and American Economic Growth: A 'Market Access' Approach." *Quarterly Journal of Economics* 131(2):799–858.

Ejdemyr, Simon, Clayton Nall, and Zach O'Keeffe. 2015. "Building Inequality: The Permanence of Infrastructure and the Limits of Democratic Representation." Working Paper. Accessed November 10, 2017. URL: *http://stanford.io/2quPaDo*

ESRI. 2008. Major Cities. In *StreetMap North America.* Redlands, CA: ESRI.

Evans, Diana. 1994. "Policy and Pork: The Use of Pork Barrel Projects to Build Coalitions in the House of Representatives." *American Journal of Political Science* 38(4):894–917.

2004. *Greasing the Wheels: Using Pork Barrel Projects to Build Majority Coalitions in Congress.* Cambridge, UK: Cambridge University Press.

Faber, Benjamin. 2014. "Trade Integration, Market Size, and Industrialization: Evidence from China's National Trunk Highway System." *Review of Economic Studies* 81(3):1046–70.

Federal Highway Administration. 2015. "Fiscal Year 2015 Computational Tables." Accessed October 25, 2015. URL: *http://bit.ly/2qODdsW*

Feldman, Stanley and Leonie Huddy. 2005. "Racial Resentment and White Opposition to Race-conscious Programs: Principles or Prejudice?" *American Journal of Political Science* 49(1):168–83.

Finifter, Ada. 1974. "The Friendship Group as a Protective Environment for Political Deviants." *American Political Science Review* 68(2):607–25.

Fischel, William. 2015. *Zoning Rules! The Economics of Land Use Regulation.* Cambridge, MA: Lincoln Institute of Land Policy.

Fitch, Catherine A. and Steven Ruggles. 2003. "Building the National Historical Geographic Information System." *Historical Methods* 36(1):41–51.

Fleming, Leonard. 2016. "RTA Transit Overhaul Millage Nears Rejection." *Detroit News* (November 8). Accessed April 11, 2017. URL: *http://detne.ws/2felAA4*

Fogel, Robert W. 1964. *Railroads and American Economic Growth: Essays in Econometric History.* Baltimore, MD: Johns Hopkins University Press.

Fogelson, Robert. 2001. *Downtown: Its Rise and Fall, 1880–1950*. New Haven, CT: Yale University Press.

Fogelson, Robert M. 1993. *The Fragmented Metropolis: Los Angeles, 1850–1930*. Berkeley, CA: University of California Press.

2005. *Bourgeois Nightmares: Suburbia, 1870–1930*. New Haven, CT: Yale University Press.

Freemark, Yonah. 2011. "Understand the Republican Party's Reluctance to Invest in Transit Infrastructure." *The Transport Politic* (January 25). Accessed November 10, 2017. URL: *http://bit.ly/2jhpb4u*

Frey, William H. 2004. The New Great Migration: Black Americans' Return to the South, 1965–2000. Technical Report Brookings Institution, Washington, DC. Accessed May 6, 2017. URL: *http://brook.gs/2pmC635*

Gainsborough, Juliet F. 2001. *Fenced Off: The Suburbanization of American Politics*. Washington, DC: Georgetown University Press.

Gallup Organization. 1983. "Gallup Poll #1207G [computer file]." Ithaca, NY: Roper Center for Public Opinion Research.

Garreau, Joel. 1991. *Edge City: Life On the New Frontier*. New York, NY: Doubleday Books.

Gentzkow, Matthew and Jesse M. Shapiro. 2011. "Ideological Segregation Online and Offline." *Quarterly Journal of Economics* 126(4): 1799–839.

Gerber, Elisabeth R., Adam Douglas Henry, and Mark Lubell. 2013. "Political Homophily and Collaboration in Regional Planning Networks." *American Journal of Political Science* 57(3):598–610.

Gerber, Elisabeth R. and Clark C. Gibson. 2009. "Balancing Regionalism and Localism: How Institutions and Incentives Shape American Transportation Policy." *American Journal of Political Science* 53(3):633–48.

Gilens, Martin. 1999. *Why Americans Hate Welfare: Race, Media, and the Politics of Anti-Poverty Policy*. Chicago, IL: University of Chicago Press.

Gimpel, James and Iris Hui. 2015. "Seeking Politically Compatible Neighbors? The Role of Neighborhood Partisan Composition in Residential Sorting." *Political Geography* 35(1):1–13.

Glaeser, Edward L. and Bryce A. Ward. 2006. "Myths and Realities of American Political Geography." *Journal of Economic Perspectives* 20(2):119–44.

2009. "The Causes and Consequences of Land Use Regulation: Evidence from Greater Boston." *Journal of Urban Economics* 65(3):265–78.

Glaeser, Edward L., Joseph Gyourko, and Raven E. Saks. 2006. "Urban Growth and Housing Supply." *Journal of Economic Geography* 6(1):71–89.

Glaeser, Edward L. and Matthew E. Kahn. 2004. "Sprawl and Urban Growth." *Handbook of Regional and Urban Economics* 4:2481–527.

Glock, Judge. 2016. "How the Federal Housing Administration Tried to Save America's Cities, 1934–1960." *Journal of Policy History* 28(2):290–317.

Goddard, Stephen B. 1994. *Getting There: The Epic Struggle Between Rail and Road in the American Century.* Chicago, IL: University of Chicago Press.

Green, Alisha. 2013. "The Landscape of Municipal Zoning Data." Sunlight Foundation. Accessed December 1, 2015. **URL:** *http://bit.ly/ 2qDEWVs*

Green, Andrew D. 2014. "County Governments and Democratic Decision Making: Explaining Why Counties Seek Approval of Local Option Sales Taxes." *State Politics & Policy Quarterly* 14(1):50–71.

Grunwald, Michael. 2015. "Overpasses: A Love Story." *Politico* (July 22). Accessed April 14, 2016. **URL:** *http://politi.co/2qDU98U*

Hainmueller, Jens, Daniel J. Hopkins, and Teppei Yamamoto. 2014. "Causal Inference in Conjoint Analysis: Understanding Multi-Dimensional Choices via Stated Preference Experiments." *Political Analysis* 22:1–30.

Hawley, Amos Henry. 1956. *The Changing Shape of Metropolitan America: Deconcentration Since 1920.* Glencoe, IL: Free Press.

Hayden, Dolores. 2003. *Building Suburbia: Green Fields and Urban Growth, 1820–2000.* New York, NY: Pantheon.

Hayward, Clarissa Rile. 2013. *How Americans Make Race: Stories, Institutions, Spaces.* New York, NY: Cambridge University Press.

Held, Tom. 2010. "Cracks Force Abrupt Closure of Zoo Interchange Bridge." *Milwaukee Journal Sentinel* (March 26). Accessed July 7, 2017. **URL:** *http://bit.ly/2sWRK6o*

Hersh, Eitan and Clayton Nall. 2016. "The Primacy of Race in the Geography of Income-Based Voting: Evidence from Public Voting Records." *American Journal of Political Science* 16(2):289–303.

Hersh, Eitan and Yair Ghitza. 2017. "Mixed Partisan Households and Electoral Participation in the United States." Working paper. Accessed July 8, 2017. **URL:** *http://bit.ly/2ttNuPg*

Hillier, Amy. 2003. "Redlining and the Homeowners' Loan Corporation." *Journal of Urban History* 29(4):394–420.

Hillygus, D. Sunshine, Seth C. McKee, and McKenzie Young. 2017. "Polls and Elections Reversal of Fortune: The Political Behavior of White Migrants to the South." *Presidential Studies Quarterly* 47(2): 354–64. Accessed May 6, 2017. **URL:** *http://bit.ly/2qDLhjO*

Hirt, Sonia. 2014. *Zoned in the USA: The Origins and Implications of American Land Use Regulation*. Ithaca, NY: Cornell University Press.

Ho, Daniel, Kosuke Imai, Gary King, and Elizabeth Stuart. 2007. "Matching as Nonparametric Preprocessing for Reducing Model Dependence in Parametric Causal Inference." *Political Analysis* 15:199–236.

Holland, Paul. 1988. "Comment: Causal Mechanism or Causal Effect: Which Is Best for Statistical Science?" *Statistical Science* 3(2):186–8.

Honaker, James, Gary King, and Matthew Blackwell. 2011. "Amelia II: A Program for Missing Data." *Journal of Statistical Software* 45(7):1–47. Accessed November 1, 2014. URL: *www.jstatsoft.org/v45/i07/*

Hopkins, Daniel J. 2014. The Increasingly United States. In *American Political Science Association Annual Meeting*. Washington, DC.

Huang, Jon, Samuel Jacoby, Michael Strickland, and K. K. Rebecca Lai. 2016. "Election 2016: Exit Polls." *New York Times* (November 8). Accessed May 20, 2017. URL: *http://nyti.ms/2qJfsDF*

Hui, Iris. 2013. "Who Is Your Preferred Neighbor? Partisan Residential Preferences and Neighborhood Satisfaction." *American Politics Research* 46(3):997–1021.

Iacus, Stefano M., Gary King, and Giuseppe Porro. 2011. "Multivariate Matching Methods That Are Monotonic Imbalance Bounding." *Journal of the American Statistical Association* 106:345–61.

Imai, Kosuke, Luke Keele, Dustin Tingley, and Teppei Yamamoto. 2011. "Unpacking the Black Box of Causality: Learning About Causal Mechanisms from Experimental and Observational Studies." *American Political Science Review* 105(4):765–89.

Iyengar, Shanto, Gaurav Sood, and Yphtach Lelkes. 2012. "Affect, Not Ideology: A Social Identity Perspective on Polarization." *Public Opinion Quarterly* 76(3):405–31. doi:10.1093/poq/nfs038.

Iyengar, Shanto and Sean Westwood. 2015. "Fear and Loathing Across Party Lines: New Evidence on Group Polarization." *American Journal of Political Science* 59(3):690–707.

Jackson, Kenneth T. 1980. "Race, Ethnicity, and Real Estate Appraisal: The Home Owners Loan Corporation and the Federal Housing Administration." *Journal of Urban History* 6(4):419–52.

Jackson, Kenneth T. 1985. *Crabgrass Frontier: The Suburbanization of the United States*. New York, NY: Oxford University Press.

Jennings, M. Kent, Gregory B. Markus, Richard G. Niemi, and Laura Stoker. 2005. *Youth–Parent Socialization Panel Study, 1965–1997: Four Waves Combined*. Ann Arbor, MI: Inter-University Consortium for Political and Social Research [producer and distributor]. Accessed October 1, 2014. URL: *http://doi.org/10.3886/ICPSR04037.v1*

Jones, David W. 2008. *Mass Motorization and Mass Transit*. Bloomington, IN: Indiana University Press.

Jordan, Jim. 2011. "Spending Reduction Act of 2011." Online. Accessed July 8, 2017. URL: *http://bit.ly/2trvogS*

Kain, John F. 1962. "The Journey-to-Work as a Determinant of Residential Location." *Papers in Regional Science* 9(1):137–60. URL: *http://bit.ly/2qE9FBN*

——— 1968. "Housing Segregation, Negro Employment, and Metropolitan Decentralization." *Quarterly Journal of Economics* 82(2):175–97.

Katznelson, Ira. 2005. *When Affirmative Action Was White: An Untold History of Racial Inequality in Twentieth-Century America*. New York, NY: W.W. Norton & Company.

——— 2013. *Fear Itself: The New Deal and the Origins of Our Time*. New York, NY: Liveright.

King, Gary and Bradley Palmquist. 1998. "The Record of American Democracy, 1984–1990." *Sociological Methods and Research* 26(3):424–7.

Kruse, Kevin M. 2005. *White Flight: Atlanta and the Making of Modern Conservatism*. Princeton, NJ: Princeton University Press.

Laing, Keith. 2015*a*. "Ryan: 'I'm against Raising the Gas Tax'." *The Hill* (June 17). Accessed December 18, 2015. URL: *http://bit.ly/2qDAh60*

——— 2015*b*. "Transit Funding Increased to Win Dem Highway Bill Votes." *The Hill* (July 23). Accessed November 10, 2017. URL: *http://bit.ly/2snbWOs*

Lee, Frances E. 2003. "Geographic Politics in the US House of Representatives: Coalition Building and Distribution of Benefits." *American Journal of Political Science* 47(4):714–28.

Leip, Dave. 2012. Dave Leip's Atlas of U.S. Presidential Elections Data File. Accessed December 15, 2012. URL: *http://tinyurl.com/kvg94p6*

Lenz, Gabriel S. 2009. "Learning and Opinion Change, Not Priming: Reconsidering the Priming Hypothesis." *American Journal of Political Science* 53(4):821–37.

Levendusky, Matthew. 2009. *The Partisan Sort: How Liberals Became Democrats and Conservatives Became Republicans*. Chicago, IL: University of Chicago Press.

Levine, Jonathan. 2006. *Zoned Out: Regulation, Markets, and Choices in Transportation and Metropolitan Land-Use*. Washington, DC: Resources for the Future Press.

Levitt, Steven D. and James M. Snyder. 1995. "Political Parties and the Distribution of Federal Outlays." *American Journal of Political Science* 39(4):958–80.

Lewis, Paul G. 1998. "Regionalism and Representation Measuring and Assessing Representation in Metropolitan Planning Organizations." *Urban Affairs Review* 33(6):839–53.

Lewis, Jeffrey B., Howard Rosenthal, Adam Boche, Aaron Rudkin, and Luke Sonnet (2017). Voteview: Congressional Roll-Call Votes Database. Accessed December 18, 2017. URL: *https://voteview.com/*

Lobao, Linda M., Gregory Hooks, and Ann R. Tickamyer, ed. 2007. *The Sociology of Spatial Inequality*. Albany, NY: SUNY Press.

Logan, John R. and Harvey Molotch. 2007. *Urban Fortunes: The Political Economy of Place*. 2nd ed. Berkeley, CA: University of California Press.

MacGillis, Alec. 2016. "The Third Rail." *Places Journal* (March). Accessed June 1, 2017. URL: *http://bit.ly/2tj7DcB*

Mashaw, Jerry L. 1971. "Welfare Reform and Local Administration of Aid to Families with Dependent Children in Virginia." 57 *Virginia Law Review* 818–39.

Massey, Douglas and Nancy Denton. 1988. "The Dimensions of Residential Segregation." *Social Forces* 67(2):281–315.

1993. *American Apartheid: Segregation and the Making of the American Underclass*. Cambridge, MA: Harvard University Press.

Massie, Thomas. 2015. Press Release: U.S. Representative Thomas Massie Introduces Bill to Secure National Road and Bridge Funding. Press release. Washington, DC. Accessed June 15, 2017. URL: *http://bit.ly/2qDTsN5*

Mayhew, David R. 2002. *America's Congress: Actions in the Public Sphere, James Madison Through Newt Gingrich*. New Haven, CT: Yale University Press.

McCarty, Nolan, Keith Poole, and Howard Rosenthal. 2006. *Polarized America: The Dance of Ideology and Unequal Riches*. Cambridge, MA: MIT Press.

2009. "Does Gerrymandering Cause Polarization?" *American Journal of Political Science* 53(3):666–80.

McGirr, Lisa. 2001. *Suburban Warriors: The Origins of the New American Right*. Princeton, NJ: Princeton University Press.

McNichol, Dan. 2006. *The Roads That Built America: The Incredible Story of the US Interstate System*. New York: Sterling Publishing Company, Inc.

McPherson, Miller, Lynn Smith-Lovin, and James M. Cook. 2001. "Birds of a Feather: Homophily in Social Networks." *Annual Reviews in Sociology* 27:415–44.

Merelman, Richard M. 1968. "On the Neo-Elitist Critique of Community Power." *American Political Science Review* 62(22):451–60.

Mettler, Suzanne. 1998. *Dividing Citizens: Gender and Federalism in New Deal Public Policy*. Ithaca, NY: Cornell University Press.

2002. "Bringing the State Back in to Civic Engagement: Policy Feedback Effects of the GI Bill for World War II Veterans." *American Political Science Review* 96(2):351–65.

Meyer, J. R., J. F. Kain, and M. Wohl. 1971. *The Urban Transportation Problem*. 4th ed. Cambridge, MA: Harvard University Press.

Michener, Jamila. 2018. *Fragmented Democracy: Federalism, Public Policy, and Political Participation*. Cambridge, UK: Cambridge University Press.

Mickle, D. Grant. 1952. "The Changing Picture in Highway Traffic." *Civil Engineering* 22:94–100.

Mieszkowski, Peter and Edwin S. Mills. 1993. "The Causes of Metropolitan Suburbanization." *Journal of Economic Perspectives* 7(3):135–47.

Mikulski, Barbara. 1970. "Who Speaks for Ethnic America? He Came in Search of Freedom and What Did He Find?" *New York Times* (September 29), p. 43.

Mitchell, Alison. 2016. Medicaids Federal Medical Assistance Percentage (FMAP). In *Congressional Research Service Report for Congress*. Accessed April 18, 2017. URL: *http://bit.ly/2oKOjPW*

Mohl, Raymond. 1993. Race and Space in the Modern City: Interstate-95 and the Black Community in Miami. In *Urban Policy in Twentieth-Century America*, ed. Arnold Hirsch and Raymond Mohl. New Brunswick, NJ: Rutgers University Press. pp. 100–58.

Mohl, Raymond A. 2002. The Interstates and the Cities: Highways, Housing and the Freeway Revolt. Technical Report. Poverty and Race Action Council, Washington, DC. Accessed June 20, 2017. URL: *http://bit.ly/2snUqNx*

2004. "Stop the Road: Freeway Revolts in American Cities." *Journal of Urban History* 30(5):674.

Molotch, Harvey. 1976. "The City as a Growth Machine: Toward a Political Economy of Place." *American Journal of Sociology* 82(2):309–32.

Monroe, Doug. 2012. "Where It All Went Wrong." *Atlanta* (August 1). Accessed July 4, 2017. URL: *http://bit.ly/2sKCDgc*

Morozov, Evgeny. 2014. *To Save Everything, Click Here: The Folly of Technological Solutionism*. New York, NY: PublicAffairs.

Moynihan, Daniel Patrick. 1960. "New Roads and Urban Chaos." *The Reporter* (April 14), pp. 13–20.

Mummolo, Jonathan. 2016. "News from the Other Side: How Topic Relevance Limits the Prevalence of Partisan Selective Exposure." *Journal of Politics* 78(3):763–73.

Mummolo, Jonathan and Clayton Nall. 2017. "Why Partisans Do Not Sort: The Constraints on Political Segregation." *Journal of Politics* 79(1): 45–59.

Mutz, Diana C. 2002. "The Consequences of Cross-Cutting Networks for Political Participation." *American Journal of Political Science* 46(2):838–55.

Nall, Clayton. 2015. "The Political Consequences of Spatial Policies: How Interstate Highways Facilitated Geographic Polarization." *Journal of Politics* 58:394–406.

Nall, Clayton, Asha Agrawal, and Hilary Nixon. 2017. "No Democratic Roads or Republican Roads: Partisanship and the Making of Transportation Policy Attitudes." *Transportation Research Board Annual Meeting.*

Nelson, Arthur, Thomas Sanchez, James Wolf, and Mary Farquhar. 2004. "Metropolitan Planning Organization Voting Structure and Transit Investment Bias: Preliminary Analysis with Social Equity Implications." *Transportation Research Record: Journal of the Transportation Research Board* (1895):1–7.

Nivola, Pietro S. 1999. *Laws of the Landscape: How Policies Shape Cities in Europe and America.* Washington, DC: Brookings Institution Press.

Office of Governor Rick Snyder. 2012. "Reinventing Michigan with Regional Transit." Accessed July 12, 2017. URL: *http://bit.ly/2tKXaVR*

Oliver, J. Eric. 2010. *The Paradoxes of Integration: Race, Neighborhood, and Civic Life in Multiethnic America.* Chicago, IL: University of Chicago Press.

Orfield, Myron. 1994. *Metropolitics: A Regional Agenda for Community and Stability.* Washington, DC: Brookings Institution Press.

O'Toole, Randal. 2010. "Fixing Transit: The Case for Privatization." *Policy Analysis* (670). Accessed November 10, 2017. URL: *http://bit.ly/2hqRH3a.*

Panagopoulos, Costas and Joshua Schank. 2007. *All Roads Lead to Congress: The $300 Billion Fight over Highway Funding.* Washington, DC: CQ Press.

Patashnik, Eric. 2000. *Putting Trust in the U.S. Budget: Federal Trust Funds and the Politics of Commitment.* Cambridge, UK: Cambridge University Press.

Patashnik, Eric M. 1997. "Unfolding Promises: Trust Funds and the Politics of Precommitment." *Political Science Quarterly* 112(3):431–52.

Patch, David. 2012. "Transit Referendums Facing Voters in 3 Local Communities." *Toledo Blade* (November 4). Accessed November 10, 2017. URL: *http://bit.ly/2hp52sJ*

Pendall, Rolf. 2000. "Local Land Use Regulation and the Chain of Exclusion." *Journal of the American Planning Association* 66(2):125–42.

Pendall, Rolf, Robert Puentes, and Jonathan Martin. 2006. "From Traditional to Reformed: A Review of Land Use Regulations in the Nation's 50 Largest Metropolitan Areas." Accessed May 26, 2016. URL: *http://brook.gs/2pSE8cm*

Peterson, Paul E. 1995. *The Price of Federalism.* 2nd ed. Washington, DC: Brookings Institution Press.

Pew Research Center. 2014. Political Polarization in the American Public. Technical Report. Accessed July 1, 2017. URL: *http://pewrsr.ch/2sdMAn0*

Pierson, Paul. 1993. "When Effect Becomes Cause: Policy Feedback and Political Change." *World Politics* 45(4):595–628.

Pisarski, Alan. 2006. Commuting in America III. Technical Report. Transportation Research Board of the National Academies. Accessed July 18, 2015. URL: *http://bit.ly/2hqQVTJ*

Policy Agendas Project. 2015. "Gallup's Most Important Problem Data." Accessed February 4, 2017. URL: *http://bit.ly/2pNs6Ta*

Polsby, Nelson W. 1968. "The Institutionalization of the US House of Representatives." *American Political Science Review* 62(1):144–68.

Pucher, John. 2004. *The Geography of Urban Transportation.* New York, NY: Guilford Press. pp. 199–236.

Pucher, John and John L. Renne. 2003. "Socioeconomics of Urban Travel: Evidence from the 2001 NHTS." *Transportation Quarterly* 57(3): 49–77.

Pucher, John R. 1998. *Consequences of the Interstate Highway System for Transit: Summary of Findings.* Vol. 42 Washington, DC: Transportation Research Board.

Puentes, Robert. 2011. "Transportation Reform of 1991 Remains Relevant." Brookings Institution. Accessed July 3, 2017. URL: *http://brook.gs/2tbHeLS*

Putnam, Robert D. 2007. "E Pluribus Unum: Diversity and Community in the Twenty-first Century." *Scandinavian Political Studies* 30(2): 137–74.

Rae, Douglas. 2001. "Viacratic America: *Plessy* on Foot v. *Brown* on Wheels." *Annual Reviews in Political Science* 4:417–38.

Rand McNally and Company. 1952. *Rand McNally Road Atlas: United States, Canada, and Mexico.* Chicago, IL: Rand McNally.

Reeves, Andrew. 2011. "Political Disaster: Unilateral Powers, Electoral Incentives, and Presidential Disaster Declarations." *Journal of Politics* 73(4):1142–51.

Reisner, Marc. 1993. *Cadillac Desert: The American West and Its Disappearing Water*. New York, NY: Penguin.

Republican Party. 2012. "Republican Party Platform of 2012." Online by Gerhard Peters and John T. Woolley. Accessed May 26, 2017. URL: *http://bit.ly/2quu9bW*

    2016. "Republican Party Platform of 2016." Online by Gerhard Peters and John T. Woolley. Accessed May 26, 2017. URL: *http://bit.ly/2quRTwu*

Riordan, William L. 1995. *Plunkitt of Tammany Hall: A Series of Very Plain Talks on Very Practical Politics*. New York, NY: Penguin.

Rodden, Jonathan. 2006. *Hamilton's Paradox: The Promise and Peril of Fiscal Federalism*. Cambridge, UK: Cambridge University Press.

    2010. "The Geographic Distribution of Political Preferences." *Annual Review of Political Science* 13:321–40.

    2018. *Why Cities Lose: Political Geography and the Representation of the Left*. New York, NY: Basic Books.

Romer, Thomas and Howard Rosenthal. 1979. "Bureaucrats Versus Voters: On the Political Economy of Resource Allocation by Direct Democracy." *Quarterly Journal of Economics* 93:563–87.

Roper Organization. 1976. "Roper Reports Poll # 1976-02." Ithaca, NY: Roper Center for Public Opinion Research.

Rose, Mark H. and Bruce E. Seely. 1990. "Getting the Interstate Highway System Built: Road Engineers and the Implementation of Public Policy, 1955–1985." *Journal of Policy History* 2(1):23–55.

Rose, Mark H. and Raymond Mohl. 2012. *Interstate: Highway Politics and Policy Since 1939*. 3rd ed. Knoxville, TN: University of Tennessee Press.

Rosenbaum, Paul. 1984. "The Consequences of Adjusting for a Concomitant Variable That Has Been Affected by the Treatment." *Journal of the Royal Statistical Society, Series A* 147(5):656–66.

Rosenbaum, Paul R. 1999. "Choice as an Alternative to Control in Observational Studies." *Statistical Science* 14(3):259–304.

Rothstein, Richard. 2017. *The Color of Law: A Forgotten History of How Our Government Segregated America*. New York, NY: Liveright.

Rubin, Donald B. 1987. *Multiple Imputation for Nonresponse in Surveys*. New York, NY: John Wiley.

    1991. "Practical Implications of Modes of Statistical Inference for Causal Effects and the Critical Role of the Assignment Mechanism." *Biometrics* 47(4):1213–34.

Salganik, Matthew and Karen E. C. Levy. 2015. "Wiki Surveys: Open and Quantifiable Social Data Collection." *PLoS ONE* 10:e0123483.

Sanchez, Thomas W. 2006. An Inherent Bias? Geographic and Racial-Ethnic Patterns of Metropolitan Planning Organization Boards. Technical Report. Washington, DC. Brookings Institution Accessed July 1, 2015. URL: *http://brook.gs/2hufgbb*

Sanchez, Thomas W., Marc Brenman, Jacinta Ma, and Richard H. Stolz. 2007. *The Right to Transportation: Moving to Equity*. Chicago, IL: American Planning Association.

Schelling, Thomas. 1971*a*. "Dynamic Models of Segregation." *Journal of Mathematical Sociology* 1(2):143–86.

1971*b*. "On the Ecology of Micromotives." *Public Interest* 25:61–98.

Schier, Steven and Todd Eberly. 2016. *Polarized: The Rise of Ideology in American Politics*. Lanham, MD: Rowman and Littlefield.

Schleuss, Jon, Joe Fox, and Priya Krishnakumar. 2017. "Did Your Neighborhood Vote to Elect Donald Trump?" *Los Angeles Times* (November 10). Accessed June 1, 2017. URL: *http://lat.ms/2tupwjI*

Schroeder, Larry D. and David L. Sjoquist. 1978. "The Rational Voter: An Analysis of Two Atlanta Referenda on Rapid Transit." *Public Choice* 33(3):27–44.

Scott, James C. 1998. *Seeing Like a State*. New Haven, CT: Yale University Press.

Seely, Bruce E. 1987. *Building the American Highway System: Engineers as Policy Makers*. Philadelphia, PA: Temple University Press.

Shafer, Byron E. and Richard Johnston. 2006. *The End of Southern Exceptionalism: Class, Race and Partisan Change in the Postwar South*. Cambridge, MA: Harvard University Press.

Skocpol, Theda. 1991. "Targeting Within Universalism: Politically Viable Policies to Combat Poverty in the United States." In *The Urban Underclass*, ed. Christopher Jencks and Paul Peterson. Washington, DC: Brookings Institution, pp. 411–36.

Smith, Tom W., Peter V. Marsden, and Michael Hout. 2015. "General Social Surveys, 1972–2014" [machine-readable data file]. Accessed August 1, 2015. URL: *http://bit.ly/2hrwpCh*

Sniderman, Paul M. and Jed Stiglitz. 2012. *The Reputational Premium: A Theory of Party Identification and Policy Reasoning*. Princeton, NJ: Princeton University Press.

Soss, Joe. 2000. *Unwanted Claims: The Politics of Participation in the US Welfare System*. Ann Arbor, MI: University of Michigan Press.

Soss, Joe, Richard C. Fording, and Sanford F. Schram. 2008. "The Color of Devolution: Race, Federalism, and the Politics of Social Control." *American Journal of Political Science* 52(3):536–53.

Stewart, Charles and Barry R. Weingast. 1992. "Stacking the Senate, Changing the Nation: Republican Rotten Boroughs, Statehood Politics, and American Political Development." *Studies in American Political Development* 6(2):223–71.

Stilgoe, John R. 1985. *Metropolitan Corridor: Railroads and the American Scene*. New Haven, CT: Yale University Press.

Stone, Clarence N. 1989. *Regime Politics: Governing Atlanta, 1946–1988*. Lawrence, KS: University Press of Kansas.

Sugrue, Thomas. 1995. "Crabgrass-Roots Politics: Race, Rights, and the Reaction against Liberalism in the Urban North, 1940–1964." *Journal of American History* 82(2):551–78.

Teaford, John C. 1979. *City and Suburb: The Political Fragmentation of Metropolitan America, 1850–1970*. Baltimore, MD: Johns Hopkins University Press.

Tesler, Michael and David O. Sears. 2010. *Obama's Race: The 2008 Election and the Dream of a Post-Racial America*. Chicago, IL: University of Chicago Press.

The Federal Aid Road Act; Summary of the. 1916. Washington, DC. Government Printing Office. Accessed June 30, 2016. **URL:** *http://bit.ly/2hodf0c*

Thurstone, L. L. 1927. "A Law of Comparative Judgment." *Psychological Review* 34(4):273–86.

Tiebout, Charles M. 1956. "A Pure Theory of Local Expenditures." *Journal of Political Economy* 64(5):416–24.

Trounstine, Jessica. 2009. "All Politics Is Local: The Reemergence of the Study of City Politics." *Perspectives on Politics* 7(3):611–18.

2015. "Segregation and Inequality in Public Goods." *American Journal of Political Science* 60(3):709–25.

2016. *Segregation by Design: Local Politics and Inequality in American Cities*. Unpublished manuscript.

United States. Bureau of Labor Statistics. 2016. *CPI Inflation Calculator*. Accessed July 15, 2016. **URL:** *www.bls.gov/data/inflation_calculator.htm*

United States. Bureau of Public Roads. 1939. Toll Roads and Free Roads. Technical Report. Washington, DC: Government Printing Office.

United States. Congressional Budget Office. 2015. Federal Housing Assistance for Low-Income Households. Technical Report. Congressional Budget Office. Washington, DC. Accessed December 16, 2016. **URL:** *http://bit.ly/2pNBJkT*

United States. Department of Commerce. Bureau of Public Roads. 1964. *Highways and Economic and Social Changes*. Washington, DC: Government Printing Office.

United States. Department of Commerce. Bureau of the Census. 1966. "1963 Census of Transportation, Vol. I Passenger Transportation Survey."

United States. Department of Transportation. Federal Highway Administration. 2017. "Interstate Highway System: The Myths." Accessed May 6, 2017. URL: *http://bit.ly/2qbkco7*

United States. Department of Transportation. Federal Highway Administration. Office of Highway Information Management. 1996. "Highway Statistics: Summary to 1995." Accessed June 28, 2015. URL: *www.fhwa.dot.gov/ohim/summary95/*

United States. Department of Transportation. Research and Innovative Technologies Administration's Bureau of Transportation Statistics. 2017. "National Transportation Statistics." Accessed June 28, 2017. URL: *http://bit.ly/2sRRngC*

United States. Public Roads Administration. 1944. Interregional Highways. Technical Report. Washington, DC: Government Printing Office. Accessed November 10, 2017. URL: *http://bit.ly/2hqH7t0*

Wachs, Martin. 2003. "Local Option Transportation Taxes: Devolution as Revolution." *ACCESS Magazine* 1(22):9–15.

Warner, Sam Bass. 1978. *Streetcar Suburbs: The Process of Growth in Boston, 1870–1900.* Cambridge, MA: Harvard University Press.

Wasserman, David. 2017. "Purple America Has All but Disappeared." *Fivethirtyeight.com.* Accessed July 5, 2017. URL: *http://53eig.ht/2tSUl57*

Weingast, Barry. 1979. "A Rational Choice Perspective on Congressional Norms." *American Journal of Political Science* 23(2):245–62.

Weingast, Barry and John Joseph Wallis. 2005. "Equilibrium Impotence: Why States and Not the National Government Financed Infrastructure Investment in the Antebellum Era." Accessed June 1, 2015. URL: *www.nber.org/papers/w11397*

Weingast, Barry R. 1994. "Reflections on Distributive Politics and Universalism." *Political Research Quarterly,* 47(2):319–27.

Weingroff, Richard. 2001. "Creating A Landmark: The Intermodal Surface Transportation Act of 1991." *Public Roads* 65(3). Accessed June 3, 2017. URL: *http://bit.ly/2rp7Vfh*

    2015. "Firing Thomas Macdonald – Twice." Accessed November 18, 2015. URL: *http://bit.ly/2qvj4aA*

Weir, Margaret. 1996. "Central Cities' Loss of Power in State Politics." *Cityscape* 2(2):23–40.

    2014. "The Politics of Spatial Inequality." In *The Cities Papers.* Brooklyn, NY: Social Science Research Council. Accessed March 26, 2016. URL: *http://bit.ly/2qDQacm*

Weir, Margaret, Harold Wolman, and Todd Swanstrom. 2005. "The Calculus of Coalitions: Cities, Suburbs, and the Metropolitan Agenda." *Urban Affairs Review* 40(6):730–60.

Weiss, Marc A. 1987. *The Rise of the Community Builders: The American Real Estate Industry and Urban Land Planning.* New York, NY: Columbia University Press.

White, Richard. 2011. *Railroaded: The Transcontinentals and the Making of Modern America.* New York, NY: W.W. Norton.

Wickert, David. 2016. "MARTA: No Longer a Dirty Word in Gwinnett?" *Atlanta Journal Constitution* (February 19). Accessed June 6, 2017. URL: *http://bit.ly/2r1CPXO*

Wiebe, Robert H. 1966. *The Search for Order, 1877–1920.* New York, NY: Hill and Wang.

Williamson, John. 2012. Federal Aid to Roads and Highways Since the 18th Century: A Legislative History. Technical Report. Congressional Research Service, Washington, DC. Accessed November 10, 2017. URL: *http://bit.ly/2hqucHi*

Wilson, William Julius. 1987. *The Truly Disadvantaged: The Inner City, the Underclass, and Public Policy.* Chicago, IL: University of Chicago Press.

1996. *When Work Disappears: The World of the New Urban Poor.* New York, NY: A.A. Knopf.

Yamada, Hiroyuki. 1972. "On the Theory of Residential Location: Accessibility, Space, Leisure, and Environmental Quality." *Papers in Regional Science* 29(1):125–35.

Yinger, John. 1986. "Measuring Racial Discrimination with Fair Housing Audits: Caught in the Act." *American Economic Review* 76(5): 881–93.

Zaller, John R. 1992. *The Nature and Origins of Mass Opinion.* New York, NY: Cambridge University Press.

Index